VIVID AWARENESS

VIVID AWARENESS

THE MIND INSTRUCTIONS OF
KHENPO GANGSHAR

KHENCHEN THRANGU

TRANSLATED AND EDITED BY
David Karma Choephel

SHAMBHALA
Boulder
2011

Shambhala Publications, Inc.
4720 Walnut Street
Boulder, Colorado 80301
www.shambhala.com

13 12 11 10 9 8 7

Printed in the United States of America

♾This edition is printed on acid-free paper that meets the
American National Standards Institute z39.48 Standard.
♻Shambhala Publications makes every effort to print on recycled paper.
For more information please visit www.shambhala.com.
Shambhala Publications is distributed worldwide
by Penguin Random House, Inc., and its subsidiaries.

Designed by Steve Dyer

LIBRARY OF CONGRESS CATALOGING-IN-PUBLICATION DATA
Thrangu, Rinpoche, 1933–
Vivid Awareness: the mind instructions of Khenpo Gangshar/Khenchen
Thrangu; translated and edited by David Karma Choephel.—1st ed.
p. cm
Includes bibliographical references and index.
ISBN 978-1-59030-816-5 (pbk.: alk. paper)
1. Mahamudra (Tantric rite). 2. Rdzogs-chen. I. Gangshar, Khenpo,
1925–1958 or 9. II. Choephel, David Karma. III. Title
BQ7699.M34T476 2011
294.3'4435—dc22
2010029800

CONTENTS

v

FOREWORD

EVER SINCE MY YOUTH, I have loved to hear stories of Khenpo Gangshar. His personality and wisdom are truly unique, and his teachings combine profound experience and complete practicality. He was a root guru to my father, Vidyadhara the Venerable Chögyam Trungpa Rinpoche, and a pivotal teacher for the Venerable Thrangu Rinpoche.

In the summer of 2001, I was able to visit Tibet and I walked and meditated in some of the meadows and caves where Khenpo Gangshar taught. I reflected on how such a great master trained his pupils in the profound view of dzogchen. This land of Tibet, with its snow-capped mountains and vast plains, is unparalleled in its beauty and ruggedness. It was in this environment that the Vidyadhara Trungpa Rinpoche and Thrangu Rinpoche received the most precious teachings that are held in the Tibetan Buddhist tradition. I'm extremely delighted that this book, *Vivid Awareness: The Mind Instructions of Khenpo Gangshar,* is available in the West, since the increase of materialism and the overwhelming power of strong emotions has not lessened since the time of Khenpo Gangshar, but has increased. He forewarned that this was a time of change, and in order to not be overwhelmed and seduced by the negativity of modern speed, it is essential to understand one's mind. This text clearly lays out the step-by-step process of how one begins that journey. The instructions contained within it are both profound and simple.

The commentary that Thrangu Rinpoche has done is both lucid and incredibly penetrating. We are fortunate to have an actual disciple of Khenpo Gangshar who has mastered these teachings to both explain and demonstrate how enlightenment can manifest in our mind and in our life. The translation itself is fluid and accessible. Thus this book is an excellent ode to Khenpo Gangshar.

One of the essential hallmarks of Khenpo Gangshar's teachings is his instruction for recognizing the nature of one's own mind. Not only does this lead to confidence in one's basic state of being, but it allows for the ability to not be swayed by the vicissitudes of life, and to remain forthright in all one's activities, constantly remaining in a state of sacredness. In order to do this, one must understand thoughts and emotions, and be able to accurately pinpoint the continuum of wisdom throughout all states of mind, whether high or low. This unfabricated wisdom is always present. This is carefully and beautifully explained in both Khenpo Gangshar's essential instructions, and by the wonderful elucidation of the Venerable Thrangu Rinpoche.

Also what is evident in this book is the unique inseparability of mahamudra and ati. These two profound traditions are one and the same. Therefore this book is an excellent guide for all of us who are traveling on the path of awakenment.

SAKYONG MIPHAM RINPOCHE
February 2010

TRANSLATOR'S
INTRODUCTION

IT IS THE NATURE of being alive that we encounter many different situations. Sometimes things go well for a while. Sometimes they don't, and we feel dissatisfaction, pain, or even misery. Sometimes things may seem good on the outside, but we still cannot find lasting happiness and comfort on the inside. This is just the nature of samsara, and it is natural to want to find relief.

This is why the Buddha taught the Dharma in general, and in particular why he taught mind instructions—instructions on how to stop turning our attention outward to all the things that distract us and elicit negative responses and instead look inside to the vivid and clear awareness that is the nature of our minds. These instructions were passed down from master to disciple in many Buddhist traditions including mahamudra and dzogchen, and every once in a while there would come a master who would adapt the instructions for their own time and situation. One such master was Khenpo Gangshar Wangpo, who in the mid-1950s foresaw the difficulties coming in Tibet and realized that he had to teach these instructions in order to help people who would soon be engulfed in turmoil. One of these people was Khenchen Thrangu Rinpoche.

Thrangu Rinpoche met Khenpo Gangshar in the summer of 1957 when Khenpo Gangshar went to Thrangu Monastery in eastern Tibet. While there, Khenpo Gangshar gave these instructions, which are a distillation of the essential points of the practices of both mahamudra and dzogchen. Later they were written down, first in a very short form and then as the slightly longer text known as "Naturally

Liberating Whatever You Meet." What makes them so beneficial for our time is that Khenpo Gangshar presents them in a way that is easy for anyone to understand and put into practice. Although many great masters, including Chögyam Trungpa Rinpoche and Tulku Urgyen Rinpoche, were students of Khenpo Gangshar, few living masters remain who heard Khenpo Gangshar give these instructions in his own voice. That makes these teachings of Thrangu Rinpoche especially precious: they are a direct and living link between ourselves and a forceful, dynamic master whose teachings benefited innumerable people in difficult times in Tibet and beyond.

In 2007, Khenchen Thrangu Rinpoche taught the mind instructions of Khenpo Gangshar on four separate occasions. Although previously Rinpoche had not often taught them, he said these were the most important teachings he had received in his life. They had been the most helpful for him during the times when he faced the greatest hardships, and Rinpoche spoke of how they could be helpful for anyone during both good times and bad. What shone through all the teachings was the depth of Rinpoche's conviction in the efficacy of these instructions and his devotion to Khenpo Gangshar.

Each time Rinpoche taught, he emphasized different points and drew on different sources not only to explain the instructions but also to show how they relate to other areas of Buddhist views and practice. This book combines all of these teachings into one thorough and complete presentation. It opens with Rinpoche's description of the history and circumstances in which Khenpo Gangshar gave these teachings, and then goes through all of the points of Khenpo Gangshar's instructions, including the general preliminary steps that we follow to prepare ourselves, the specific preliminaries of investigating what the mind is like, the actual main practice of resting within the nature of the mind, and the follow-through instructions on taking all of the different situations we encounter in our lives as the path so that we can nurture our recognition of the nature of mind and not be overwhelmed by transient circumstances of our lives and deaths. Drawing on all different areas of Buddhist philosophy and quoting from memory and from many great masters and texts (which can make it difficult to find a source for every citation),

Rinpoche explains everything clearly and simply so that these instructions will be helpful to new and old practitioners alike.

In this translation, I have used the word *intelligence* to translate the Tibetan word *shes rab* (Skt. *prajñā*) and *wisdom* to translate *ye shes* (*jñāna*). The actual meaning of *shes rab* or *prajñā* is the discernment that can distinguish what is from what is not, and its usage in many texts as well as in common speech is more akin to the English word *intelligence*. Although the word *prajñā* is frequently used in English translations, when people hear it, there is a tendency to think of prajñā as something special, different, and extraordinary—something that we don't ordinarily have but need to get through spiritual practice. Actually, it is a quality that is inherent in every consciousness we experience; we just need to sharpen and develop it through listening, contemplating, and meditating, so it seems better to use an ordinary English word to indicate this.

I would like to thank the people whose efforts made this book possible, including Erik Pema Kunsang for his gracious assistance and permission to use his translation of Khenpo Gangshar's "Naturally Liberating Whatever You Meet," Alexis Shaw and the Orange County Vajra Vidya Study Group for transcribing the teachings, and the many others who have had a hand in making Khenpo Gangshar's texts available and producing this book.

I hope that all of you who read this book find that practicing these instructions gives you tangible benefits in this life; I hope it brings you to the ultimate, enduring happiness of buddhahood. May this book be a cause for all to bring the greatest benefit to themselves and others.

DAVID KARMA CHOEPHEL
Thrangu Dharmakara Translations

PREFACE

THESE DAYS, THERE ARE many people who want to recognize the nature of the mind and practice meditation on it, and there are also many lamas who point out the nature of the mind. For this reason, I thought it would be especially beneficial if there were some mind instructions to help these people.

The instructions in this book were first taught orally by the great scholar and meditation master Khenpo Gangshar Wangpo. He first wrote them down in a very short text, which he then elaborated on in the longer text called "Naturally Liberating Whatever You Meet." But the era in which Khenpo Gangshar lived and wrote this text was a time of great conflict and there was a danger that it would be lost in the turmoil. Perhaps it is a sign of the merit of his students, or perhaps the result of his own activity, that his instructions were not lost. It is very fortunate indeed that they were preserved and remain in this world.

Now these instructions have been translated into English, and I have full confidence that they will be able help many people all over the world. These instructions are not just for academic study; they focus on practice. They are a way to tame the greed, aversion, and delusion in your mind and bring yourself mental peace and happiness so that you will be able to help yourself and others. I ask you to please put them to good use.

PART ONE

HELPFUL ADVICE
FOR GOOD TIMES
AND BAD

LONG AGO, MARPA THE TRANSLATOR AND MANY OTHER Tibetans went to India to study and learn the Dharma. They made the difficult journey to India, studied with great masters, meditated, and really learned the Dharma. When they returned to Tibet, they taught the instructions they had learned, and so the Dharma spread widely in Tibet, where it has flourished until the present day. As a result of this, we are now able to enjoy and make use of the Dharma. We can study it and contemplate its meaning. We can do meditation practice. Our opportunity to do all this comes out of the great kindness of all those great translators and masters of the past.

Now you have a similar intention to learn something about the Dharma. You did not pick up this book to read some great story or learn how to be successful in business and get rich. The only motivation you could possibly have is to learn about the Dharma. It is not always easy to study Dharma—you might face some difficulties, financial or otherwise. But studying and practicing the Dharma is something that will be very helpful to you and many others for generations to come. It will help the Dharma spread in your own country and flourish for many hundreds of years to come. This is wonderful.

Whenever we study the Dharma or do any Dharma practice, the most important thing is to have a pure motivation. If we have a pure motivation, whatever we do with our body, speech, and mind will turn out well. But if our motivation is not pure, then even if what we do with our body, speech, and mind seems good from the outside, it will actually not turn out well in the end. Just starting to read this book shows that you want to learn about the Dharma and to practice it; it demonstrates that you have some faith and devotion. This is a good motivation, but it is important to have a truly vast motivation—the motivation of bodhichitta. Sometimes our motivation is influenced by our afflictions, and if that is the case, then we should get rid of such a motivation. Sometimes our motivation is not in any way afflicted or negative, but it is possible that it is just a wish to help ourselves. There is nothing terribly wrong about that sort of motivation, but it is very limited, and so this also is a motivation that we should give up. Instead we should have the motivation to bring benefit to all of our former mothers and to all the sentient beings of all six realms of samsara who are as limitless as space. It is for their benefit that we practice the Dharma. It is for their benefit that we need to study the Dharma, so please read these teachings with the pure motivation of bodhichitta. This is the best reason to practice the Dharma.

1

PROPHECIES OF
HIDDEN LANDS

THE TOPIC OF THIS BOOK is some instructions given by a khenpo from modern times, Khenpo Gangshar. I received them directly from Khenpo Gangshar himself and I found them very helpful at that time. I met him and received these instructions in August of 1957, which was the beginning of the period when I faced the greatest difficulties and dangers of my life.

The situation in Kham, the area of eastern Tibet where I am from, grew steadily worse throughout 1957 and 1958, and just over a year after receiving these instructions I had to leave my homeland and flee Tibet. During that period I faced the danger of losing my life or being thrown in prison. There were great hardships, too: sometimes we had no food, sometimes we had no clothing or no place to stay. I encountered my enemies, and when that happened, the most beneficial Dharma for me was this particular teaching. Remembering these instructions and keeping them in mind was extremely helpful for me.

When we think about what happens internally when we experience such difficulties and suffering, we see that there is a danger that anger, jealousy, or another negative emotion will arise in our minds. The reason these profound instructions were so helpful for me at that time is that they are the antidote for anger, jealousy, and all the other afflictions. If at that point I had gotten angry, I might have joined the war and fought against the Chinese. Many people told me I should become a general and lead an army to fight a big battle. Had I done so, there would have been the possibility of killing many people or committing other misdeeds, and later I would have looked back on it with regret. I would have thought, "That was not good. I killed a lot of people. I did something terribly wrong and in the end this will turn out badly." There could have been no happiness in my life. But because of these instructions, I felt no anger, and so I did no wrong-doing. I did not kill anyone, prepare to kill anyone, or even form the intention to kill. That was because of this Dharma teaching. I used these instructions as my companion in sorrow and suffering, and because of that I was able to avoid losing control of myself to the afflictions. This is the great help that these instructions gave me.

When I look back on those times, I think about how I faced both the danger of my enemies and the danger of accumulating bad karma. There was a danger that I could have gone down the wrong path. But I was able to meet some great lamas, and because of their kindness and the instructions they gave me, I think things actually turned out rather well. I was not overcome by the afflictions and did not accumulate any bad karma. Even though at that time I experienced many difficulties and faced many dangers, I did not conceive of them as difficulties or dangers. I feel good about this.

When anger arises in us, there is a danger that we will be mistaken in the moment. We might start to fight, or we might say something harsh or unpleasant that we will regret in the future. Thus it is important that we take control of our minds. If we reduce the intensity of the afflictions, it is extremely helpful, and in the future we will be able to think, "Things actually worked out back then."

I have heard other people say similar things, including Beru Sherab Palden, who lives at Samye Ling in Scotland. At that time, Sherab Palden was in Lhasa, and he heard that war had broken out in Tibet. One day he hid himself within a house, looking out through a window. He had a good rifle and saw that he had a good shot on a Chinese soldier. He had the thought, "I should kill that Chinese," and so he aimed at the soldier. He could have shot at any moment, but then he thought, "No, how can I kill a person? That is no good." He then put the gun away. Later he said that this was actually very good fortune that he did not shoot and kill anyone. It was the kindness of the Three Jewels that stopped him. In the same way it is important for you to keep control over your mind. If you manage to do so, things will turn out for you as well.

It is quite possible that there will be times when everything is happy, peaceful, and wonderful in your life, but it is also possible that there will be times when you are unhappy, face difficulties, and experience a lot of suffering. During the times when you are happy, there is a danger that you will fall under the control of your afflictions, and there is a similar danger during times when you are unhappy. What we need at such times is Dharma practice. When you are experiencing suffering and when you are experiencing happiness, you need practice and instructions as a friend in times of need. Doing this practice has been helpful for me in my life, and I hope that it will be helpful for you, too, in both good times and bad.

WHERE THESE INSTRUCTIONS CAME FROM

The profound instructions presented in this book are rather new. There are instructions that were given thousands of years ago when the Buddha appeared in this world and that the Buddha actually spoke with his own mouth. There are also all the instructions from the great meditators and great scholars of India. Similarly, there are the words of the great scholars and meditators who appeared in Tibet both during the initial spread of the ancient Nyingma tradition and later during the spread of the newer Sarma tradition. But these instructions are not any of those. These only appeared very recently. The person who taught them, Khenpo Gangshar Wangpo, was a great scholar who later became a mahasiddha. Looking into the future, he saw that in 1958 and 1959 the situation would become very difficult. He saw that Buddhism would come under attack and that many people would experience great hardship. He saw that Dharma practitioners would face many obstacles. He gave these profound instructions so that they would not be harmed by these difficulties and so that they would not suffer.

Khenpo Gangshar was born into the family of the Shechen Gyaltsap Gyurme Pema Namgyal, who was one of the main teachers at the Shechen Monastery in Kham. The Shechen Gyaltsap's main teacher, from whom he received many teachings directly, was Jamgön Kongtrul Lodrö Thaye, the great nonsectarian nineteenth-century master who compiled all of the teachings of Tibetan Buddhism into the *Five Great Treasuries*. One of the Shechen Gyaltsap's nephews was the great scholar Khenchen Lodrö Rabsel, with whom I studied the sutra teachings when I was in monastic college. These studies included the abhidharma, the middle way, the vinaya, validity and logic, and so forth. The Shechen Gyaltsap also had a niece named Otso, who was Khenpo Gangshar's mother. She gave birth to him in the Wood-Ox year, 1925.

When he was a young boy, Khenpo Gangshar met the Shechen Kongtrul Rinpoche, one of the reincarnations of Jamgön Kongtrul Lodrö Thaye. The Shechen Kongtrul recognized him as an emanation of a great Indian master and said that he would become an exceptional person, so he should be well cared for, but no one believed this because actually he was quite naughty and rough—they doubted any child so badly behaved could possibly become someone exceptional. But at some point his potential was awakened and he began to study and practice the Dharma. He became quite learned and was appointed as a khenpo of Shechen Monastery. He also developed a very deep and strong meditation practice. Later, when he began to give his own particular instructions, which lead to really exceptional experiences, people recognized what an exceptional lama he was.

Khenpo Gangshar gave these instructions just before the bad times came to Tibet. At that time, some people got ready to fight, saying that it was necessary to struggle and resist, but Khenpo Gangshar did not agree: he said that to fight would be barbaric and would be contradictory to the Dharma. Our motivation to fight could only be an unvirtuous motivation sparked by hatred and jealousy. Such a motivation is inappropriate for Buddhists and could not bring any good. It would only bring us harm, not only in this life but in our future lives as well. In particular, if monks were to go to war, this would destroy the teachings of the Buddha. This would not be something that anyone else had done—we would have destroyed Buddhism ourselves, he said. That could not possibly be the right thing to do.

So what did he say we should do at that time? He said that the Dharma is not something outside of ourselves. It is inside us, so practicing within ourselves is the most beneficial thing to do. Buddhism does not depend on external things; it depends on taming our own minds. If we tame our own minds, Buddhism will not disappear. At that time in Tibet and later during the Cultural Revolution, if you were to say OM MANI PADME HŪM, there was a danger that someone might turn you in. But Dharma does not depend upon that. Taming our own minds alone is the genuine Dharma. We needed to act in accordance with the Dharma. We needed to be patient. We needed to be compassionate and have a kind heart. And the best and most important way to develop this kind heart is to follow these special instructions on looking at the nature of the mind.

Several years earlier, the Tenth Trungpa Rinpoche, Chökyi Nyinche, had gone to Shechen Monastery and formed a good connection with the Shechen Kongtrul Rinpoche. Because of this, when the Eleventh Trungpa tulku, Chögyam Trungpa Rinpoche, needed to receive the empowerments, instructions, and transmissions for the *Five Treasuries* of Jamgön Kongtrul Lodrö Thaye—*The Treasury of Terma, The Treasury of Spiritual Instructions, The Treasury of Kagyu Mantra, The Treasury of Knowledge,* and *The Treasury of the Vast Word*—he invited Shechen Kongtrul Rinpoche to Surmang Dutsi Til Monastery and received *The Treasury of Spiritual Instructions* from him. Later Trungpa Rinpoche went down to Shechen Monastery and received *The Treasury of Terma* and *The Treasury of Kagyu Instructions.* Following that, he decided to start a shedra at Surmang Dutsi Til Monastery and needed to invite a khenpo. The khenpo he invited was Khenpo Gangshar. At that time, Khenpo Gangshar was not in very good health, but he thought it would be beneficial for beings and the teachings, so he went. He taught Trungpa Rinpoche *The Supreme Continuum* and middle-way philosophy. While teaching *The Supreme Continuum,* he fell ill, and at that time a verse came to him, which he wrote down:

Within the first month, *Zing zing zing!*
Within the second, *Ururu!*
Within the third month, *Sharara!*
Within the fourth month, *Trarara!*
Within the fifth month, wails of *Sharara!*
Within the sixth, the Chinese shout *So!* will ring out.
Within the seventh, they'll control the realm of Tibet.
If on the cusp of the fifth, seventh, and sixth,
You do not go to a hidden land, delaying,
There is no doubt you will be made Chinese.

His students said this sounded like a prophecy, but he said it was nothing. He did not think of himself as a great meditator or teacher. He did not see himself as having pure perception or being able to make prophecies, so he threw it into a fire, but the paper flew back out unharmed. This is how he made the prophecy.

The meaning of his prophecy was that the situation would get worse and worse throughout the first sixth months of the Tibetan lunar calendar, but there would be a time in the fifth, sixth, and seventh lunar months—the three months of summer—when we could flee to the hidden lands. If we did not make it there, it would be very bad. But where were the hidden lands that we should flee to? The hidden lands are not lands that are outside of us in any respect, he said. The hidden lands refer to knowing the nature of our mind well. It is important that our minds not be overcome by the afflictions or suffering. The hidden lands are not outside of ourselves; they are our own minds.

These hidden lands had also been prophesied by Guru Rinpoche, who had said that there were four hidden lands: Lotus Array in Assam; Khenpa Jong, which is in Bhutan; the Land of Rice or Sikkim; and Yolmo Ganggi Rawa in Nepal. The prophecy says that those who go there will be able to arrive, and that when we reach the hidden lands, we will reach the pure lands of the dharmakaya, enjoyment body, and emanation body. At that time, some people said that the Tibetans should flee to the four hidden lands prophesied by Guru Rinpoche. But how could this be possible? If our minds are filled by the afflictions and obscurations and we have spent the first part of our lives performing misdeeds and unvirtuous acts, it is not possible that we could simply travel by foot and somehow arrive in a pure realm of the dharmakaya or an enjoyment body. There is no way we could get there. But that does not mean that Guru Rinpoche's prophecy is false.

What Guru Rinpoche's prophecy says is that when we want to go to the hidden lands, first we will come to a great river. We could try many different ways to cross it, but we will not find any way to cross it except for one. What is this one way? On the banks of the river there grows a great tree. We need to chop the tree down, but it cannot be felled by any ordinary axe or saw. So how can we chop it down? We need to dig at the base of the tree, and there at its very root we will find a crystal axe. We can use this crystal axe to fell the tree, and when we do, it will fall across the river, becoming a bridge that we can walk across. This is how we will be able to cross the river and reach the pure land of a dharmakaya, enjoyment body, or emanation body.

We should not take the words of this prophecy too literally—otherwise it would be impossible. How is it possible that there is a river that cannot be crossed? And how could there be some tree that cannot be cut by steel? It is not possible. Even if there were such a tree, if it could not be cut by steel, how is it that a crystal axe could cut it? If we whacked such a tree with a crystal axe, the axe would shatter on the first blow. This is just not plausible. One cannot simply fell a tree and walk across it to a pure land. Khenpo Gangshar said that the words of the prophecy were actually quite good, but we have to read them symbolically, not literally. So what does the great river mean? It is the great river of samsara, filled with the afflictions and our bad karma. It is something we must cross, but how? We need a method, and that method is the tree on the riverbank. What does the tree represent? It is the tree of clinging to a self. We need to cut down this tree of ego-clinging, which means we need to get rid of it. But after we have chopped it down, it becomes something we can use—this is what we call "taking ego-clinging as the path." We can practice relative bodhichitta, saying, "I am going to attain buddhahood in order to bring benefit to all sentient beings." Then we can take our ego-clinging as the path and use it as a bridge to cross the river of samsara and arrive in the great city of omniscience and freedom.

We cannot chop down the tree of ego-clinging and make it into a bridge in the ordinary way. But if we dig next at its roots, we will find intelligence that realizes the lack of a self. That intelligence is the crystal axe. The only place you can find it is at the base of the tree of ego-clinging. If we find that intelligence, realize that the self actually has no essence, and look at what the nature of the self really is, that is the crystal axe. We can then use this crystal axe of the intelligence that realizes selflessness to cut down the tree. Once we have cut down the tree of ego-clinging, we can take it as the path to cross the river of samsara. That is how we can reach the pure realms of the dharmkaya, enjoyment bodies, and emanation bodies. Khenpo Gangshar stressed that this means that it is critical for us to practice meditation—it is on the basis of our practice that we will be able to reach the hidden lands.

There are many different types of instructions on how to practice, but they can be primarily classified into two types: practices that require effort and practices that are effortless. The instructions that require effort include such things as accumulating merit, gathering a sangha of monks and nuns, and building temples. But these would have been impossible at that time and place. It would have been foolish even to make plans to do so. So what did we need to do at that time? We needed to tame our own minds.

There are many different ways to tame our mind. There are many things we can do—engage in creation-stage deity practices, recite liturgies, recite mantras, use our bodies to accumulate merit, and so forth. However, many of these are things that we would not have had the power to do at that time. What we did have the power to do was to take control of our mind. This is something that can be done anywhere, in any situation. If we can practice these instructions on taking control of our mind, we will not have any suffering, we will not experience any fear, and there will be no problem of doing any misdeeds. There will not be any difficulties. This is what Khenpo Gangshar said when he gave these instructions, which turned out to be extremely helpful for many people.

I went back to Tibet in the 1980s, and while I was there I met many lamas, monks, and Dharma teachers. Many of them had spent over twenty years in prison camps undergoing tremendous physical suffering. But many of them had also met Khenpo Gangshar and received his profound instructions. They were able to contemplate these extraordinary instructions, develop renunciation and world-weariness, and practice. They tried to take control of their minds and practice the instructions as much as they could in prison. The more they practiced, the more beneficial the instructions were for them. Their practice went well, and as a result they did not find their situation so difficult. Similarly, many people fled Tibet and went to India. Fleeing was extremely difficult—there were many worries, great fear, and many hardships. But these instructions were helpful for them, too.

Our situation nowadays is not like that. We do not have so many difficulties. We do not have to practice the Dharma in secret. We can do creation-stage practices if we want. We can do completion-stage practices if we want. We can study the Dharma if we want. But Khenpo Gangshar said that we should consider these oral instructions on recognizing the nature of our minds especially important. They can help us all individually: when we have temporary difficulties and temporary suffering, they can directly help us to deal with those problems. Not only that, but if we practice them, they will bring great blessings and power that will make it possible for us to achieve the ultimate result of buddhahood. They are therefore helpful in both the short and long terms. That is why he said that these are such excellent and wonderful instructions.

TERTÖNS AND TREASURES

Generally speaking, all Dharma is the same in essence, but each different instruction has its own particular time and place. A Dharma teaching that is the most appropriate instruction for a particular time and place is especially helpful and has especially great blessings. This is the reason why Guru Rinpoche, the great Indian master who was instrumental in bringing the Dharma to Tibet, hid so many Dharma teachings as treasures (termas). Guru Rinpoche traveled all over Tibet hiding these treasures in cliffs, lakes, and other places so that they could be found at the time when they would be most helpful and would have the most power. Then hundreds of years later a tertön—a treasure discoverer—would appear and find the instructions at the time when they were most appropriate.

Khenpo Gangshar, as he said himself, was a tertön. There are many different types of tertöns who have appeared through the centuries, and they discovered their treasures in many different ways. Some found material treasures and others found Dharma treasures. Those who found material treasures would find symbolic items such as a vajra, a phurba, an unusual statue, or some other object in a cliff, beneath a lake bed, or in another such location. With Dharma treasures, many discovered what are called "yellow papers." Yellow papers are the documents that had been written down by Yeshe Tsogyal, Guru Rinpoche's consort, who wrote quite a few of these treasures in tiny letters. When tertöns would discover such a treasure, they would copy it down. These are some of the ways tertöns have found treasures.

Although Khenpo Gangshar was a tertön, he was a different kind of tertön. He did not find external objects, texts, or anything like that. He said himself that he was not someone who revealed treasures from external things. Instead, he found the treasure of the nature of his own mind within. This made him an extraordinary type of tertön.

Khenpo Gangshar's main student was Chögyam Trungpa Rinpoche. One day, when Khenpo Gangshar was giving a teaching at Thrangu Monastery, he told us a story about how Trungpa Rinpoche wore some jewels—one or two stones or crystals wrapped in a cloth—around his neck. The previous Trungpa tulkus had all worn these jewels around their necks, and the Eleventh Trungpa also wore them.

One day when he was young, Chögyam Trungpa Rinpoche took a day off. He went to a mountain stream, took off his clothes, and went for a swim in the river. When he came out, he had lost the jewels and could not find them. The jewels remained lost for one or two years until Khenpo Gangshar Rinpoche came to Surmang Dutsi Til Monastery and gave him some profound instructions. Through these

instructions, Chögyam Trungpa Rinpoche developed exceptional realization within himself—and during that time he happened to go
back to the river—and find the jewels.

There were several different explanations as to why the Trungpa
tulkus wore these jewels. Some said that they wore the jewels as some
sort of a protection from difficulties, ghosts, or spirits, but that is
not the real reason. Some people said that these jewels would protect
the Trungpa tulkus from weapons, but that also is not the reason.
The real reason they wore them is that the jewels represent the jewel
of the mind, which is always present within ourselves. Wearing the
jewels was a sign of having meditated on the nature of the mind, and
of having developed realization about how the mind is. This is the
reason why the successive incarnations of the Trungpa lineage wore
these jewels around their neck. Just as the previous Trungpa tulkus
had realized the nature of their minds, so too the subsequent incarnations realized the nature of their minds and wore the jewels as a
symbol of that.

Just like his predecessors, Chögyam Trungpa Rinpoche wore these
jewels. But people and their situations are always changing, and when
Chögyam Trungpa was young, he forgot the nature of his mind and
the way the dharma nature is. That is when he lost the jewels. Later
he received Khenpo Gangshar's profound advice and was able to realize the nature of his mind, and that is when he found the jewels.

All of the various incarnations of the Trungpa tulku lineage were
exceptional beings with exceptional realization, but sometimes great
lamas forget things when they take a new body. The reason is that
they have exchanged bodies. For example, if in your own life you
develop a problem with your brain, you might forget something you
used to know. Great lamas did not just have a problem with their
brain—they exchanged their old brain for an entirely new one! They
have an entirely new body. They have not lost their internal qualities,
but they have not yet redeveloped the wisdom. This is why when
great lamas are young they still need to sit down and learn the al-
phabet. They have a new body and need to develop their qualities,
but you can tell even at an early age that this is someone with great
intelligence and great wisdom. This is someone whose experience

will naturally blossom and develop. This is just the nature of inter-dependence.

Khenpo Gangshar discovered the treasures of the mind by help-ing students to realize the nature of their own minds—the cause of liberation and omniscience that is present as the essence of their own mind stream. We have not yet recognized the nature of our minds, so he gave his instructions as a way for us to come to know it. In this way he discovered the wish-fulfilling jewel of the mind. This is the sense in which Khenpo Gangshar was a tertön: he gave instructions on the nature of the mind.

KHENPO GANSHAR'S VISIT TO THRANGU MONASTERY

Khenpo Ganshar first gave these instructions at Surmang Monastery in the summer of 1957. Then he sent an elderly monk from Surmang named Karma Ngödrup to go around in advance and give the mes-sage to people that Khenpo Gangshar would be giving his teachings everywhere and that everyone should come—these were important and timely teachings.

A few days later, Khenpo Gangshar came to our monastery and gave his teachings. He went to teach everywhere—he went up to the retreat center, down to the shedra, to the main monastery, and down to the town. He taught the Dharma and gave his instructions to every-one he met. He told them that they must practice the Dharma well and that even though there was a great danger from the Chinese, they must not fight. It was wrong to kill, he said. Instead they should take control of their minds. Khenpo Gangshar first taught these instruc-tions orally, and then he composed the very short and pithy set of instructions titled "The Concise Mind Instructions Called Naturally Liberating Whatever You Meet" while staying at the retreat center at Thrangu Monastery. Later he expanded these instructions into the somewhat longer text titled "Naturally Liberating Whatever You Meet." The instructions in that text are essentially the instructions that he taught while staying at Thrangu Monastery. These instruc-tions are short but carry exceptional blessings and power. Not only are they beneficial, they are also easy to practice. They are concise yet profound and can truly help us. In them, Khenpo Gangshar reveals the jewel of the nature of the mind that is already present within us.

Khenpo Gangshar gave his instructions in many different ways, including through poetry and metaphor. There was a monk at Thrangu Monastery who was in retreat and asked Khenpo Gangshar for some advice. Khenpo Gangshar replied with a poem, which said that sitting on the peak of a rocky mountain was a vulture. Sometimes the vulture soared up high in the sky, and sometimes it floated down to the ground. In the end, though, the vulture just dies. "Do you understand this instruction?" asked Khenpo Gangshar.

This particular monk had studied quite a lot. "Yes, I do," he replied. "The rocky mountain is our pride. On the pinnacle of this mountain, the vulture represents great intelligence. This is like a high view—the view of realizing emptiness and forceful reasoning. Sometimes the view soars like a vulture higher and higher, and sometimes it comes down to the ground. But if you don't actually practice the Dharma, one day the vulture will just die. Flying around high in the sky does not help much if one day you are just going to die anyway." This is how Khenpo Gangshar taught the importance of meditation practice. Sometimes we have a high view but do not practice much. This is what the vulture represents: sometimes we spout high views with our mouths, saying lofty and difficult words such as "There is no self" or "Emptiness," words that soar ever higher and higher. But after the vulture soars up and up and up, it eventually comes down to the earth, and after it lands, what does it do? Being a vulture, it eats carrion, whether a horse's corpse, a human corpse, or the corpse of some other animal. Eventually, it will die in some miserable fashion. Similarly, having high views will not help us much in the end. What really helps us is practice.

If all we do is think about it conceptually, then it is perhaps a bit difficult to see the essence of the mind as it is. But if you have strong faith and devotion as well as renunciation and weariness with the world, then it is possible for you to realize the nature of mind. If your faith and devotion are not all that strong, then even if you put a lot of effort into it, it will be somewhat difficult. This is why it is important to reflect upon how fortunate we are to have a precious human body and how fortunate it is to have entered the gate of the Dharma. It is extremely important to study and contemplate this, to generate faith and devotion, and develop our wonderful ability.

The Buddha taught eighty-four thousand different types of Dharma. What is the root of all of all the eight-four thousand different Dharma teachings? In the terms of the foundation vehicle, it all comes down to the selflessness of the individual. Because we cling strongly to a self, the afflictions arise. Because of these afflictions, we then experience many different types of suffering. In order to free ourselves of that suffering, we need to get rid of the afflictions. In order to abandon the afflictions, we need to realize the selflessness of the individual. For that reason, the foundation vehicle teaches meditation on the selflessness of the individual.

The great vehicle teaches not just the selflessness of the individual, but also the selflessness of all phenomena. The great works of middle-way philosophy use logic to teach that all phenomena are empty. They teach the sixteen different types of emptiness and so forth to show us how to discard the strong fixations we have. In order to discard our fixations, we need to realize the way things truly are. In order to realize that, we need to develop certainty through logical analysis, which can then bring us to a realization of emptiness.

When we do the practices of the secret mantra vajrayana, we do not just strive to realize the selflessness of the individual, nor do we merely try to come to an understanding of the emptiness of all phenomena. We do try to understand these, but we do not use these practices as the basis of our meditation. So what do practitioners of the secret mantra do? Primarily, we do the practices of mahamudra and dzogchen. In these practices we do not look out at external phenomena, but look inside to get to the bottom of the way our mind is so that we can realize the nature of our mind. We see that it is empty; we examine the way the mind actually is. When we see the nature of our mind, we can pacify all of our excessive clinging and our strong feelings. These practices are a wonderful way to tame our fixation.

Whether we are practicing mahamudra or dzogchen, the fundamental method is to look at the nature of our mind and realize it, naked, just as it is. This is the technique that Khenpo Gangshar's instructions teach. These methods and instructions are very important to consider, both in the ultimate terms of Dharma and in the temporary terms of this world. The reason is that they can help us in both good times and bad.

There are some people who are happy and do not have any problems. Everything goes as it should and they are happy, healthy, and joyful. But what happens to us when we become happy, healthy, and joyful? Often our thinking gets confused. As it is said, external phenomena are too bright, and our internal mind is not bright enough. As a result of this, we forget to think about our ultimate purposes and forget to practice the Dharma. But we must not forget to practice. We need to be able to practice meditating on the nature of mind, and if we do so, our practice will go well. This is why it is important to practice the Dharma when things go well.

Sometimes people encounter many problems in their lives. There are many obstacles, things go wrong and they feel like they cannot get anything done—everything goes badly. When that happens, we are often overwhelmed by suffering and feel sorry for ourselves, thinking "I'm having a hard time." But there is no point to doing that. Other people have difficulties with strong negative emotions and afflictions that occur. We should not be surprised and dumbfounded if there are some problems in our lives. Our practice can help us in such times: if we meditate on these instructions, it will help us, so that we will not feel such suffering.

Whether we are happy or unhappy, it is important that we contemplate the nature of our minds. If we can practice in this way, it will be like the saying on mind training:

> In happy times, it bows our neck;
> When bad times come, it is a friend.

When things are good, meditating on the nature of the mind will prevent us from playing too many games. When times are bad, we won't wallow in despair and depression. If we meditate on the nature of our mind, we will not have such a hard time and things will go well; this is extremely helpful.

Khenpo Gangshar was a lama unlike any other. I did not know much about him before he came to Thrangu Monastery. When he was about to arrive, many people said that he had the best instructions and strongest and most powerful blessings, and when I heard that, I thought I was going to receive those blessings, too. But when he came, I did not feel anything special on the first day. I did not feel anything on the second day. I was disappointed, but people had said that you get his blessings through his mind instructions, so I decided to ask for them. When he gave me the instructions, at first I did not feel anything. But a few days later, while I was eating my supper, I had this feeling and suddenly realized, "This is what the lama was talking about! This is what he meant!" I experienced a feeling unlike any other I had ever felt, and that is when I realized what an extraordinary lama he was and how powerful his teachings were. That is how it happened.

After giving his instructions at Thrangu Monastery, Khenpo Gangshar left, accompanied by Trungpa Rinpoche. They headed toward Shechen Monastery, but Trungpa Rinpoche was turned back at the border between the districts of Qinghai and Sechuan by the Chinese, and Khenpo Gangshar continued on his own. I heard that later nothing particularly bad happened to him. He passed away peacefully after an illness; he did not die in a Chinese prison. This is what I heard, but I never met anyone who could confirm this.

2

RECOGNIZING OUR
GOOD FORTUNE

THE TITLE OF THESE INSTRUCTIONS is "Naturally Liberating Whatever You Meet: Instructions to Guide You on the Profound Path." These instructions are intended to guide us down a profound and helpful path. They are instructions that we need to encounter and when we do, we receive their great blessings and power. Because of that, everything that we meet can be naturally liberated. This is why they are called "Naturally Liberating Whatever You Meet."

There are many wonderful instructions in Tibetan Buddhism, including the mahamudra instructions of the Kagyu tradition and the dzogchen instructions of the Nyingma tradition. But Khenpo Gangshar's text does not give a complete presentation of the instructions on mahamudra, nor does it give a complete presentation of the instructions on dzogchen. Instead, Khenpo Gangshar presents the most fundamental instructions of both mahamudra and dzogchen. He uses mahamudra terminology such as "ordinary mind" and dzogchen terminology such as "differentiating mind and awareness." Thus this text is a summary of all the mind instructions of mahamudra and dzogchen. It is especially connected with the Kagyu lineage because Khenpo Gangshar was a student of Shechen Kongtrul Rinpoche, who was a student of the Shechen Gyaltsap Gyurme Pema Namgyel. The Shechen Gyaltsap was himself a principle disciple of Jamgön Kongtrul Lodrö Thaye, a master of the Kagyu lineage.

Khenpo Gangshar begins these instructions by paying homage so that they can be helpful for many people. The text reads:

> With the devotion of self-knowing I pay homage to Guru Vajradhara.

The homage, or prostration, is to Guru Vajradhara. The fact that we are able to meet someone who can give these instructions and our great fortune to be able to receive them depend upon Vajradhara— they depend upon the nature of the mind. This is something that we can meditate upon if we want. If we want instructions on it, we can receive them. That is why we pay homage to the Guru Vajradhara.

In general, there are said to be four different kinds of gurus. The first is the individual guru of the lineage. Individual gurus of the lineage are all the lamas who have appeared one after another in the lineage. The second type of guru is the word guru of the sugatas. This means the speech of the Buddha and the instructions of all the great adepts. We can read these in books and come to understand them so that we can develop some experience of what they teach. The third type of guru is the sign guru of appearances. When we meditate, we gain some experience through our practice, and as we continue, we see various appearances. These are the sign guru of appearances: as we see them through the experience of our practice, our experience grows clearer and clearer. The fourth type of guru is the ultimate guru of the dharma nature. This means that as we do our meditation practice, there is something we can meditate on, something we can come to realize and experience. There is a result to attain through practice. All appearances arise out of the nature of our minds, and there is something in the nature of the mind to recognize. That is called the ultimate guru of the dharma nature. Of these four different gurus, here we are prostrating to the fourth, the ultimate guru of the dharma nature. We can meditate, and by doing that we will gradually develop experience and exceptional realization. This is called Guru Vajradhara, the dharmakaya Vajradhara who is within the ultimate nature.

Many of us have seen pictures of Vajradhara, and we think of him as being blue in color, with two hands and holding a bell and a vajra.

That form is the enjoyment body of Vajradhara. The Vajradhara we prostrate to here, however, cannot be found to have any form. Vajra means unchanging—the unchanging dharma expanse or nature of phenomena. The ultimate nature is something that we can experience and practice. There is something we can realize, and as we practice we can attain to the ultimate results of the practice. That is why we prostrate to it.

The manner in which we prostrate is with the devotion of self-awareness. Here what is important is that we are paying homage with our own self-awareness and with the devotion present in our mind. Normally when we think of prostrations, we think of what we do with our body: first joining our palms and then bending down, putting our hands, knees, and head on the ground. We think of this physical action as being a prostration, but that is not what is meant here. What is really meant here is that we feel faith and excitement in our minds about the ultimate guru of the dharma nature. We think, "I can experience this. I'm going to meditate and practice. By doing so, I am going to realize what there is to realize." We prostrate mentally with respect, faith, and belief in both the Dharma and these instructions.

The Tibetan word for prostration is *chhaktsal*. The first syllable, *chhak,* means to sweep or clean—to clean up all the dust. Meditating is a bit like cleaning: we want to find the nature of our mind, but it is hidden by all our coarse afflictions and bad thoughts. The meaning of the syllable *chhak* is that we are sweeping away those obscurations. The second syllable, *tsal,* means to request something. It is like saying, "I am going to meditate, and through doing the practice I would like to realize the nature of the mind." This is a prayer to realize the nature of the mind.

Worthiness and Good Fortune

After the prostration, Khenpo Gangshar begins the instructions with a description of a worthy or fortunate student:

> A worthy student is one who aspires to practice the profoundest of the profound and secret vajrayana—the

essential oral instructions of all the anuttara yoga tantras or the nature of the realization of effortless ati.

The Buddha gave several different types of teachings because he taught the Dharma that was right for each individual student and met their needs. There are in general three different types of teachings: the vehicle for listeners, the vehicle for bodhisattvas, and the vehicle of the secret mantra vajrayana. Of these three vehicles, the instructions here come from the secret mantra vajrayana because that is the vehicle that is easiest to practice and brings the greatest benefit.

In the secret mantra vajrayana, there are four different classes of tantras: action tantra, conduct tantra, yoga tantra, and unexcelled (*anuttara*) yoga tantra. Dharma practitioners in Tibet do some practices from the action tantra and the yoga tantra, but they primarily practice the fourth class, the unexcelled yoga tantra. Khenpo Gangshar's instructions present the main or essential instructions — the most important points or the essence of the unexcelled yoga.

There are many different practices within the unexcelled yoga tantra, which can be summed up as practices that involve effort and those that do not involve effort. Those that involve effort are such practices as the six yogas of Naropa within the tradition of mahamudra. These are the meditations on tummo, transference of consciousness, illusory body, and so forth. Within the dzogchen tradition, there are the instructions on thögal, which sometimes involve practicing in darkness and sometimes practicing in sunlight, and so forth. All of these practices involve effort.

The oral instructions of the unexcelled yoga tantra also include effortless practices that are easy to do. In the mahamudra tradition, these are taken from the nondual tantras, which are the last of the three sections of the unexcelled yoga tantra. In the context of dzogchen, the effortless instructions are called ati yoga, or the effortless ati. This means dzogchen, the great perfection. The Third Karmapa Rangjung Dorje described the great perfection in his "Aspiration Prayer of Mahamudra":

This freedom from mental engagement is mahamudra.
Beyond extremes, it is the great middle way.
As this includes everything, it is also called the great
  perfection.
May we gain the confidence that to know one is to realize
  the meaning of all.

What this means is that when we are practicing without any particular mental engagement—when we are not strictly paying attention
to something—and we are looking at the nature of the mind, that is
mahamudra. We can call it by other names as well. Since it is free of
all the extremes of permanence or nihilism, it is in the middle, so it
is also called the great middle way. Because it is the perfection of all
meanings, it is the great perfection, or dzogchen. The aspiration is
that we may have the confidence that by knowing one, the nature of
the mind, we may know all: mahamudra is just this; great perfection
is just this; the great middle way is just this. This is what is called here
the effortless ati of the great perfection.

When the great meditation masters of Tibet teach these instructions, they call them "mind instructions." If we say "dzogchen," we
mean mind instructions. If we say "mahamudra," we mean mind instructions. What we mean by mind instructions is that we don't really
analyze external appearances. We instead look directly at the nature
of our internal mind itself. When we see that, the emptiness of all
phenomena is just that. The clear knowing aspect is just that. We are
able to recognize this, and so that is what we mean by mind instructions: meditating on our minds.

Because mind instructions are effortless, they are easy to practice and fit into any lifestyle, as the examples of the eighty-four
mahasiddhas of India show. Some of the mahasiddhas were great
scholars and did this practice simultaneously with their intellectual work. Others were not so well educated but were still able to
do this practice. Some were very wealthy and had a lot of possessions, yet were still able to do this practice. Still others led simple,
uncomplicated lives with few possessions and were also able to do

this practice. This is because these instructions are effortless, easy, and uncomplicated. These instructions are intended for people who want to enter the gate into the practice of mahamudra and dzogchen, for people who think to themselves, "I want and need to do this practice."

Khenpo Gangshar says his instructions are meant for worthy or fortunate students. This is very important: you are a fortunate and worthy student—you are extraordinary in this regard. Even if the Dharma spreads throughout the world and is preserved, if you are not fortunate, you will not be able to practice them. For example, in Asia the Dharma is close and conditions are good. All you need to practice Dharma is here: there are places to study the Dharma and practice the Dharma. There are many opportunities. Yet even so, many people do not have the fortune to take advantage of this. Dharma is close, available, and important for them to practice, but they are not inclined to practice and their minds are distracted by worldly affairs when they should be looking up toward the Dharma. Such people are not fortunate.

In contrast, many Westerners will travel long distances, crossing great oceans just to study and practice the Dharma. Even those who stay in their own country often now have the interest and ability to practice. You are very fortunate to be able to encounter the Dharma at this particular time and to have the wish to practice it. For example, if you had been born seventy years earlier, you would not have had the opportunity to encounter the Dharma because at that time it was almost impossible to even hear of the Dharma, let alone encounter it. Even those Westerners who encountered the Dharma at that time often did not have the wish to practice it. For example, there was an Englishman named Francis Younghusband who went to Lhasa in 1904. Of course the Dharma flourished in Lhasa, but his motivation did not intersect with the Dharma. He thought of the Dharma as stupid and was more interested in politics and power. Maybe he thought of Tibetans as ignorant and thought more of politics. Perhaps he had a better motivation and thought that he would need to help the poor Tibetans by teaching them his own modern, sensible ways, but in any case his motivation prevented him from actually encountering the Dharma. He was powerful and influential, but he did not have the fortune to practice the Dharma.

When I first traveled to the West, there were people who had some faith in the Dharma, but they often had doubts about some things. Most people wanted to hear certain types of Dharma teachings, but often they were not interested in receiving empowerments or did not know that they should take empowerments. They believed some Dharma teachings but doubted others. Nowadays as the Dharma spreads and becomes popular in the West, people are developing a stronger belief in the Dharma. Some people even have complete faith in the Dharma, which is excellent.

But even though the Dharma has spread to many lands, not everyone is able to enter the gate of the Dharma and practice it. Not everyone is able to believe the Dharma. Even many who have started to learn about the Dharma and begun to believe it are unable to practice it. But you are not like that: you have fortune to be able to practice the Dharma. Over the course of many aeons, you have gathered a tremendous amount of merit, because of which you now have had the good fortune to be born in a precious human body, encounter the Dharma, and recognize how valuable it is. You have seen how the Dharma will be beneficial for your life and have developed faith in it. Not only do you have faith, but you actually have the wish to practice the Dharma. Such an intention is actually very difficult to come by. This is a wonderful, great fortune, and this is what it means to be a worthy student. Now that you have this good fortune, it is important that you be diligent in your Dharma practice.

Joy and Excitement for Our Practice

It is important to realize how fortunate we are. Sometimes we forget and think to ourselves, "Well, I've started practicing Dharma but I haven't had any signs of experience or realization." We might get depressed or discouraged about it, but there is really no need for that. We have entered the gate of the Dharma and are what is here called a worthy student. We should recognize this for the good fortune that it is. We should remember that practicing the Dharma is good and beneficial, and reflect on how lucky we are to be able to practice it.

When we are receiving instructions, it is important that we have faith and devotion, and the most important thing for that is to be really excited. We need to realize how fortunate we are to be able to do this. If we really see how fortunate we are, this will be really wonderful and extremely beneficial for us. But if we have this great fortune and instead of recognizing it we think it is something ordinary, we will not be able to extract much power out of the instructions. This is why the great teacher Shantideva said:

> Those who thus with clear intelligence
> Take hold of the awakened mind with clear and lucid joy,
> That they may now increase what they have gained
> Should lift their hearts with praises such as these.

We need to be joyful and excited, because if we feel enthusiasm for our practice, we will be more and more diligent. Then our practice will just get better and better. On the other hand, if we are not excited about our practice and do not have any joy for it, it will not really go anywhere. Similarly, in order to confess and get rid of our wrongdoings, nonvirtues, and negativities, we should regret them and think, "Oh, that was not so good." If we do that, they will naturally decrease. Otherwise, if we think, "That was great!" they will grow stronger and stronger. Therefore we should always be excited and happy about our Dharma practice and regret our misdeeds and nonvirtues.

Sometimes we set the foundation for our Dharma practice by generating weariness with the world. We think about the impermanence of all phenomena. We think about suffering. By doing that, we develop world-weariness, and from that we recognize that we really need to practice the Dharma. Out of that recognition, we begin to actually practice the Dharma. Sometimes when we practice, we do not worry about developing world-weariness. Instead, we have joy and excitement. We think about how fortunate we are to be able to practice. Now that we have this good fortune, it is important to practice. These are two different methods of inspiring ourselves to practice, one through world-weariness and the other through joy and excitement. The method we should use now is to generate joy and excitement.

This is not merely a question of feeling joy and excitement within our minds. We need to contemplate how extremely fortunate we are to be able to practice the Dharma in this world now. The Dharma of the great vehicle has spread. The Dharma of the Theravada tradition has also spread. The Dharma of the secret mantra vajrayana has spread. These three different types of Dharma have all appeared in this world. Since I am someone who practices the secret mantra, it is a bit uncomfortable to say that the vajrayana is the best of these three types of Dharma, but this is in fact the case. It is important to know what is right and true. We have this great fortune: the secret mantra vajrayana flourished in Tibet and then spread beyond. Now we have all the favorable conditions we need to practice the Dharma. The instructions are here, and we have the opportunity to practice the best Dharma.

When the Buddha appeared in India, he taught the Dharma and had many followers—arhats and mahasiddhas—who preserved and protected the Dharma. They practiced the Dharma and passed on the oral instructions for their practices. All of these instructions were preserved in their entirety in Tibet. But they were not just preserved as mere words or intellectual knowledge; the great masters practiced these instructions and many of them achieved realization through the instructions. All of these instructions have been preserved in Tibet without deteriorating or being lost. In terms of external circumstances, there have been some difficulties, but in terms of the internal practice, the essence of all the spiritual instructions that were given and preserved in India and then spread to Tibet has not encountered any obstacles. These instructions have been maintained in an unbroken continuum in Tibet. We are very fortunate that the Dharma that the Buddha taught has not been lost but has been preserved.

In the ninth century, there was a Tibetan king named Langdarma who tried to eradicate the Dharma in Tibet. He destroyed many temples and tried to stamp out the Dharma, but he did not succeed. The lineages of the Dharma and the instructions were preserved through that period. If we look at recent history, there was the Cultural Revolution in Tibet. But even during the Cultural Revolution, the Dharma did not disappear. They destroyed temples, tore down statues, and burned sacred texts, but the lineage of the Dharma was not lost. That lineage of the Dharma still exists and you as a Dharma practitioner have the great fortune to read these teachings. You have the opportunity to practice and should remember this great fortune.

The great teacher Patrul Rinpoche told a story that illustrates how we should practice. Once there was a blind man who was stranded alone in the middle of a vast plain. He did not know where he was. He did not have any helpers. He could not tell which direction was east or west; there was no way he could go anywhere for help. Since he was blind, there was no way for him to know where to go. While he was wondering what he would do, he heard the sound of a cow grazing, munching on grass, and had a brilliant idea: "I can grab the cow's tail and follow that cow home, and there will be someone there to help me." He listened to the sound of the cow masticating, stumbled over to it, and grabbed its tail. He hung on as tight as he could and would not let go, following the cow wherever it went as it wandered across the plain. Finally, it returned to its owner's house, and the blind man found someone who could help him out of his situation.

In a sense, we are in a similar situation, stuck in samsara, but we have now found the path of the Dharma. Just like the blind man who hung on to that cow's tail for dear life, we need to hold on to the Dharma as tight as we can. If we do so and continue to practice, we will be able to achieve the ultimate result of this effort. Perhaps it is not such a good idea for me to compare you to a blind man being dragged hither and thither by a cow, but now that you have this good fortune to find the Dharma, you should hang on to it tight. Practice the Dharma, and you will reach the highest results.

Now we have encountered a really profound instruction. Not only is it a very special instruction, it is one we can actually practice. We also have the wish and intention to practice it. We have an opportunity to study it. What a wonderful great fortune this is! If we realize what a great fortune we have and we are joyous and excited about it, it will eventually bring us to a wonderful result. So for that reason I ask you to please be as excited and joyous about this as you can.

3

THE GENERAL
PRELIMINARIES

THESE INSTRUCTIONS have three different parts. The first is the preliminary steps of mind training. We all have minds, and the nature of our minds is naturally completely pure and excellent. But we have come under the power of confused relative appearances, so we need to train, purify, and cleanse our mind. The process of cleansing and training our minds is the preliminary practice.

The second step is the main practice of pointing out. We need to have the nature of mind pointed out to us, and we need to recognize it, as will be described below.

The third instruction is the subsequent application, combining the profound advice into key points. What do we need to do after we have recognized the nature of mind? We need to take these instructions as the path, and apply them. When we encounter suffering, we need to be able to get rid of our suffering. When we experience fear, we need to be able to get rid of our fear. When we experience attachment, clinging, and the afflictions, or when we experience torpor and agitation, we need to be able to get rid of them. We can use these instructions to deal with these and take them as the path. This is the subsequent application that combines the profound advice into key points.

There are many different types of Dharma instructions and practices. For the listeners, practitioners of the foundation vehicle, the main practice is to give up nonvirtue and maintain good behavior, through which they come to achieve a good result. The great vehicle includes practices of relative and ultimate bodhichitta. The main practices of relative bodhichitta are to give up our bad habits of mind and replace them with good thought patterns such as the wish to help all beings. The main practice of ultimate bodhichitta is to try to realize the meaning of the emptiness of all phenomena.

But in the secret mantra vajrayana, the main practice rests upon the fact that all our pleasures, suffering, confusion, and qualities come down to our mind, and so we need to understand what the essence of the mind is. We put particular emphasis on the mind because if we realize its nature, it will be as if everything else is transformed as well. If we can really get to the bottom of the mind, we can take control over everything. The three sections of these instructions are all methods to apply this focus to the mind.

The preliminary steps of mind training are divided into two sections: the general preliminaries and the special preliminaries, which represent the unique qualities of this particular path. Although it does not say so in the text, the first of these also has two parts: the common preliminaries of the four thoughts that turn the mind and the uncommon preliminaries of going for refuge, arousing bodhichitta, and so forth. The first part, the common preliminaries, is not explicitly taught in the text, but it is very important for these instructions.

THE COMMON PRELIMINARIES

People often say to me that they like the Dharma in general. They have faith in the Dharma; they believe in it, but sometimes they are unable to practice. They ask me what the best thing to do in this situation is. We need to realize that practice is something we cannot do without. We need to think about the reasons why Dharma is indispensable. If we think about the reasons, faith will come, and then we will naturally become diligent in our practice. This is why we contemplate the nature of things and the four thoughts that turn the mind.

The First Thought

The first thought that turns the mind is the contemplation of the precious human body, so difficult to find. We are very fortunate to have this precious human body and we should not let it go to waste. It is very important to realize this. But it is not just that we have a human body—we are also extremely fortunate to have encountered these instructions. Khenpo Gangshar was a great meditator from a remote and isolated region of Tibet. He gave these instructions in that area, and if you think about it, it is next to impossible that you could have encountered them. He taught them in a place very far away, and eventually they were translated into English so that now you can read them. But just having the possibility of reading the instructions is not in and of itself a good fortune. You might have thought, "It's just a book by some crazy lama from Tibet. Why should I pay any attention to it? What good is practicing this going to do? I'm from America! I'm really smart! I don't need this crazy Tibetan guy's instructions at all." Although you could have thought that, you did not. Instead you thought, "These are important. If I study them and put them into practice, they will help me." You have some faith in them. Thus these instructions were taught in an isolated region of Tibet, gradually spread, and were translated into English. Then you came across them and developed faith and interest in them. What an incredible good fortune! This good fortune to encounter the Dharma and these particular instructions is the precious human birth, so difficult to find. We have encountered the Dharma, which is so hard to find. When we encounter the Dharma, we need to be able to have faith and devotion, and we have been able to do that. Now that we have such good fortune, we must not let it go to waste—we need to practice in this human life.

The Second Thought

The second thought that turns the mind is the contemplation of death and impermanence. Sometimes we think of this as being depressing. It is an unhappy and unpleasant topic. But this weariness does not hurt us in any way—it helps us. As the Buddha said, "At first it is the condition that encourages us toward the Dharma. In the middle, it is the rod that spurs us on to diligence. In the end, it is the companion of the result."

When we say that it is a condition that encourages toward the Dharma, this means that at first, when we haven't thought about impermanence, during happy times we get distracted by our pleasure. But our happiness always changes in the end. Its nature is impermanent. If we do not know this and get distracted, in the future, when it changes, it will be as if there is nothing we can do and we will be badly off. If we start thinking about impermanence now, we can prepare ourselves well. This will encourage us to practice the Dharma; we will think, "I must practice." We will not forget the Dharma.

Once we are motivated to practice the Dharma, how does contemplating impermanence help? In the middle, it is the rod that spurs us on to diligence. Sometimes we might start feeling a bit lazy, but if we have contemplated impermanence we will feel as if we can't let ourselves be lazy. We will think that we need to be diligent.

In the end, meditating on impermanence is the companion for attaining the result. What this means is that first it encourages us to practice the Dharma, then it encourages us to be diligent, and in the end we achieve a wonderful result. As Milarepa said,

> First I went to the mountains out of fear of death,
> But now I've seized the stronghold of deathlessness.

In the beginning, Milarepa went to the mountains and meditated out of a fear of death. As a result of that, he reached a state beyond the fear of death. If we practice in the same way as Milarepa, this can happen for us as well, but even if we cannot accomplish as much as Milarepa did, we can feel as if we have done something. This gives us confidence. If all we do is recite a hundred OM MANI PADME HŪM mantras with a kind heart and good motivation, at least we can think, "On that day I really recited those *mani*s well." We will be pleased with what we have done. Even if a virtuous act is small, it will not go to waste and will be very helpful.

The Third Thought

The third thought that turns the mind is the contemplation of karma. We often think that karma means we do not have any control, but it is not really like that. Actually, karma gives us control. We all want to be happy, but we wonder whether that is possible. It is possible: if we perform the cause of happiness—virtuous actions—we will experience the happiness that results from them. Similarly, we do not want to suffer. Can we get rid of suffering? Yes, we can, because the cause of suffering is misdeeds and nonvirtue. If we give those up, we will gain freedom from suffering. Therefore if we properly take up virtue and give up wrongdoing, we can be happy and free of suffering.

The Fourth Thought

The fourth thought that turns the mind is meditation on the defects of samsara. We humans experience the suffering of birth, aging, sickness, and death. We encounter difficulties and obstacles. Ordinary people think that they are just having hard luck and that only they are having these problems, but that is not how it is. Birth, aging, sickness, death, and all kinds of problems are characteristics of samsara. Everyone experiences them. This is why we need to practice Dharma. By practicing Dharma, we can abandon the afflictions. By abandoning the afflictions, we can give up misdeeds and nonvirtue, which will bring us freedom from suffering. To free ourselves from samsara, we need to practice the genuine Dharma, and to do that we primarily need to practice meditation. This is why we meditate on the defects of samsara.

Thus the general preliminaries are to contemplate the four thoughts that turn the mind: the precious human body; impermanence; karma, cause and effect; and the defects of samsara. If we understand them and their reasons thoroughly, we will naturally enter the Dharma and be diligent about it. These common preliminaries allow us to enter the Dharma even if we had been unable to before.

THE UNCOMMON PRELIMINARIES

Next, the text explicitly describes the four uncommon preliminary practices. The first of these is refuge and bodhichitta:

> Taking refuge, which is the difference between this path and an incorrect path. Arousing bodhichitta, which raises you above the inferior paths.

In general, the wish to enter the gate of the Dharma is really quite rare. But even if we develop such a wish, there is a danger that we will follow a wrong path. We might not even know that it is the wrong path. How can we avoid the wrong path? We need to take refuge in the Three Jewels of the Buddha, Dharma, and Sangha. We take refuge in the Buddha Shakyamuni as the teacher. The path we need to follow is the Dharma that he taught, and our companions as we practice this path are the Sangha. In the secret mantra vajrayana, we also go for refuge in the root of blessings, the guru; the root of accomplishment, the yidam deities; and the root of activity, the Dharma protectors. Although in general we go for refuge in the Buddha, Dharma, and Sangha, the one from whom we receive the power and blessings of the Buddha is our root guru, which is why the guru is called the root of blessings. We also need to accomplish the Dharma, and we do this primarily through the creation and completion-stage practices of a yidam deity, which is why yidam deities are called the root of accomplishment. We take refuge in the Sangha in general, but some members of the Sangha take a human form while others do not. Those who appear in a nonhuman form are great bodhisattvas manifesting as Dharma protectors, so we make offerings to them and invoke them to perform various types of activities. This is how we go for refuge in the three roots. When we do the practice of going for refuge in the Three Jewels and the three roots, we recite the prayer of going for refuge, and also prostrate a hundred thousand times. This is the practice of taking refuge, which marks the difference between this path and the incorrect path.

We need to practice and accomplish the Dharma. Normally, our motivation for doing this is to help ourselves or, if we have a slightly larger motivation, to help a few other people. The motivation to truly help other people is extremely rare, and the motivation to bring benefit to all sentient beings almost never happens, but it is extremely important. Whether we are doing Dharma or worldly work, thinking only of our own benefit may be a good motivation, but it is very limited and narrow. Similarly, if our motivation is to benefit a select few other people, that too is a good motivation, but it is also limited. The motivation that we really need is broader and more spacious—the wish to bring benefit to all sentient beings. All sentient beings want to be happy; all sentient beings want to be free of suffering, and therefore we need to bring them to happiness and free them from suffering. The power to be able to do this comes from practicing the Dharma. That is why we study and practice the Dharma—so that we can attain the ultimate result and be able to help all sentient beings in the future. It is important for us to develop this vast intention of bodhichitta. If we have a limited motivation, the results that we achieve will also be limited. But if we have a vast motivation, the results that we attain will be vast. That is why when we embark upon the path, it is important to develop the bodhichitta that raises you above the inferior path.

Vajrasattva

The second of the preliminaries is:

> The meditation and recitation of Vajrasattva, which purifies misdeeds, obscurations, and adverse conditions that prevent the essence of refuge and bodhichitta from dawning in your being.

Why do we do Vajrasattva meditation? We often have many problems that prevent us from developing relative and ultimate bodhichitta, the meditation that realizes the nature of the mind. What are these problems? Often they are the obstacles from bad acts that we have committed in previous lives. These are what we call misdeeds. We also often have strong imprints from the past that lead us to have strong afflictions and coarse thoughts. These are what we call obscurations. Often we have thoughts of greed, aversion, delusion, pride, or jealousy. These are what we call the afflictive obscurations. Sometimes, we might not experience greed, aversion, jealousy, or another affliction, but we have many thoughts that prevent us from practicing meditation. These are cognitive obscurations. We need to purify ourselves of all these misdeeds and obscurations. Generally we would apply mindfulness and awareness and confess our misdeeds, but that is the common path. In the uncommon practices of the secret mantra, we meditate on Vajrasattva above the crown of our head because he is the lord of all the buddha families. Then amrita flows from his heart and into our bodies, filling us. This purifies all the illness in our bodies and all the misdeeds and obscurations in our minds.

Sometimes we might practice tranquility meditation. We might be enthusiastic about doing it, but sometimes we have a lot of problems. Our mind will not rest as it is: it is not clear and many thoughts keep arising. We are not able to develop good tranquility meditation. When we want to tackle this problem directly, we apply mindfulness, awareness, and carefulness. We look to see if we have any agitation or dullness. We apply the remedies for those. We look to see if there are a lot of thoughts in our mind, and we apply the remedies for those. But sometimes it is better to do this indirectly rather than directly, and that is when we do the meditation on Vajrasattva and visualize that all the imprints from previous lives that prevent us from developing stable tranquility meditation are pacified. This will help our tranquility meditation.

Sometimes when we do visualization practices of the creation stage, we have trouble visualizing clearly and our minds will not rest. This problem can happen, and the main method for getting rid of it is diligence, but Vajrasattva meditation will purify our imprints and help us in practices of the creation stage. It is also helpful with insight meditation. Sometimes our insight meditation is clear and good, but sometimes it is unstable. When their insight meditation is not clear or stable, many people ask me what they should do. One thing we can do is Vajrasattva practice, which, by purifying our misdeeds and obscurations, is very helpful. All of this is why we do Vajrasattva practice.

When we do Vajrasattva practice, we can do the visualization and think that we are doing it to purify all our misdeeds and obscurations in general. But we can also think that we are doing it to purify a particular problem. If we often get very angry or jealous, for example, we can do Vajrasattva meditation to purify that. If we have a particular problem in our meditation, we do Vajrasattva practice to purify that problem. When we do the visualization, we visualize nectar flowing out of Vajrasattva's body and into us. As it flows into us, we think that it is purifying that specific problem: it is purifying our anger, our jealousy, or the particular problem in our meditation. We think that the blessings of Vajrasattva are purifying that very problem. This is a particular benefit of the meditation on Vajrasattva.

We need something very sharp to purify our misdeeds and obscurations. Resting in naturalness is very loose and relaxed. It has great blessings and the power of the dharma nature, but because it is so relaxed, it does not have the sharpness we need to purify misdeeds and obscurations. When we are trying to purify ourselves, we need to have the intention to confess and purify our misdeeds. The repetition of the hundred-syllable mantra and the visualization of nectar flowing through ourselves and purifying us of our misdeeds and obscurations give Vajrasattva practice the sharp edge and power that purify us of our misdeeds.

It is like when you get sick. There are some medicines that work in a very slow and gentle way, such as ayurvedic or homeopathic medicine. If you take these medicines, they will gradually help you feel better. But sometimes you have a particular thing that hurts, and it is better to have an operation. The surgeon cuts the thing that hurts out of you and then you can get better quickly. Vajrasattva practice is like surgery that directly removes the root of the problem.

Mandala Offerings

This preliminary practice of Vajrasattva may dispel all our adverse conditions and problems, but we still might find ourselves in a position where our meditation is not progressing or developing. The reason is that not all conditions are adverse conditions; there are also favorable conditions. If we have purified all the adverse conditions but have not developed the favorable conditions, things will not go so well. Therefore we need to develop the favorable conditions, which are the accumulation of merit. If we have the support of the vast accumulation of merit, we will be able to truly develop realization within ourselves. Our meditation will go very well and we will not have any difficulties.

If we are doing the visualization stages of the creation stage, we will have clear visualizations and our practice will go well, without any difficulties. That is why the third preliminary is to accumulate merit by making mandala offerings. As Khenpo Gangshar describes:

> The mandala offering, which is the method for gathering
> the accumulations—the harmonious conditions.

In order to accumulate merit, we need to be generous. We need to make offerings to the Three Jewels and be generous to the unfortunate. Generally, we cannot actually give material things on such a large scale, but in the secret mantra vajrayana, there is another method of giving, which is to make mandala offerings. Offerings and generosity usually mean giving actual things, but the most important thing is the mind. As Shantideva says in *The Way of the Bodhisattva*:

> Transcendent giving, so the teachings say,
> Consists in the intention to bestow on every being
> All one owns, together with the fruits of such a gift.
> It is indeed a matter of the mind itself.

It is the good and kind thought, "I am going to make a gift" that is generosity, whether or not we actually give something. So when we make mandala offerings to accumulate merit, we do not take actual things and offer them. Instead we make vast offerings with our mind—we have a vast mental motivation. We imagine that we are taking the entire world along with all of its riches and prosperity and everything else, and offer it to all the buddhas and bodhisattvas. When we do this, we are able to accumulate vast amounts of merit.

Gathering merit is an important point. Sometimes we have the right circumstances and our Dharma practice goes well. Sometimes we find ourselves in unfavorable circumstances, and it can be difficult. We need to do something to have more of the good conditions. We need to get rid of bad or even just average conditions. The way to develop and increase favorable situations is to gather merit. In the sutras, it says that the Buddha had to gather merit for three uncountable aeons—a huge and vast accumulation of merit over an extremely long period of time. In the secret mantra vajrayana, it is not necessary to gather quite so much merit, but we absolutely must practice both the accumulation of merit, which has a focus, and the accumulation of wisdom, which does not have a particular focus.

Guru Yoga

Finally, in order to generate experience and realization quickly, we do the practice of guru yoga, which is a way to receive the blessings of the practice. As Khenpo Gangshar says,

> Guru yoga, the root of blessings and the means by which
> the special qualities of experience and realization quickly
> arise in your being.

Once we have gotten rid of any adverse conditions and assembled the favorable ones, we need to develop experience and realization quickly. The way to do this is as mentioned in the "Short Vajradhara Lineage Prayer," which says, "Devotion is the head of meditation." We need to supplicate the lama and develop faith and devotion in him or her. If we have the faith and belief that we need to practice the lama's instructions, we will be able to truly develop high realization.

We need to develop in our beings and our Dharma practice. We need to develop our samadhi meditation. We need to develop the creation stage of the deities and the completion stage. Through these we need to develop experience and realization. The general method for doing this is to be diligent, have pure perception, and develop devotion. But instead of doing that directly, we might want an indirect method, and that is the practice of praying to the root and lineage gurus through the practice of guru yoga. When we do guru yoga, we develop devotion in our beings. But what is devotion? At first, we are able to develop our meditation. Then we will be able to practice guru yoga, and through our practice we will develop faith and devotion. This will make us more diligent, and then we will be able to receive greater blessings.

Sometimes people think that blessings are something that will make them shake, tremble, and even levitate. But that is not what blessings are. Blessings are the power of the Dharma. When we encounter the power of the Dharma, we start to feel faith, and then we become diligent. We feel love and compassion, and we develop tranquility and insight. This is what blessings are. They are the absence of greed, aversion, and delusion. If we can entirely rid ourselves of those three things right away, that is wonderful, but even if not, we can decrease and suppress them. That is blessings.

In general, blessings come from the Buddha, but we cannot meet the Buddha directly and we cannot hear him teach. Does this mean that we cannot practice? It does not. We can practice just as if we could meet and listen to the Buddha, because the blessings of the Buddha were passed on to the lineage lamas, who have passed them on to our root lamas. Our root lamas now give these blessings to us. This why the root lama is the root of blessings.

Since we need to develop faith and supplicate the lamas, we do the practice of guru yoga so that we can receive the lamas' blessings. When we receive greater blessings, it is easier for us to develop true experience and realization.

So these are the general preliminaries: refuge, bodhichitta, Vajrasattva, mandala, and guru yoga. We practice these "according to the general teachings." This means that we need to practice them continually.

PART TWO

THE SPECIAL PRELIMINARIES: THE ANALYTIC MEDITATION OF A PANDITA

FOLLOWING THE GENERAL PRELIMINARIES COME THE special preliminaries, which according to this system of teachings are called "the analytic meditation of a pandita." Khenpo Gangshar's instructions teach two different ways to meditate: the analytic meditation of a pandita and the resting meditation of a kusulu. When we say "analytic meditation of a pandita," *pandita* means a scholar—someone who is learned, examines phenomena, and develops intelligence. This develops the power of their intelligence so that they are able to see the nature of things as they are. When we say "resting meditation of a kusulu," *kusulu* basically means someone who takes it easy and does not spend much time worrying about anything. Kusulus just sit down and get right to meditation without thinking things through too much. So the resting meditation of a kusulu is a meditation where there aren't all that many thoughts and you just look directly at the nature of the mind. Of these two, the analytic meditation of the pandita is presented here as the preliminary, and the resting meditation of a kusulu is presented as the main practice.

The text first discusses the analytic meditation of the pandita. Analytic meditation here does not mean to just analyze through logic and inference. Of course we are analyzing, but here we look at the nature of the mind to see what is it like. Experiencing that and fully comprehending it is the analytic meditation of the pandita.

There is a difference between this analytic meditation of the pandita and the use of the logic and reasoning of the middle way to come to a comprehension of emptiness. The distinction is that in the practices of the middle way, one uses only inference in order to examine how things are, and through this one develops certainty. You can come to see that all phenomena are emptiness: all external phenomena are emptiness and the internal mind is emptiness. This is a method that leads to certainty of the emptiness of all phenomena, but since that certainty is conceptually fabricated, it is difficult to develop an actual experience of emptiness and the nature of phenomena. In the analytic meditation of the pandita, however, we do not use inference to analyze and examine. We use our experience to see where the mind is, what it is like, and what its essence is. This brings us not only to certainty, but to an actual experience of what the mind is like. This is the analytic meditation of the pandita.

4

THE FOUNDATION
KARMA, CAUSE, AND RESULT

THE DISCUSSION OF KARMA, cause, and result that opens the text is the basis for all the instructions that follow. It is important for us to believe in karma, cause, and result. There are different kinds of people. Some people naturally have faith in the existence of past and future lives. They naturally have faith in karma, cause, and result. If you are one of these people, that is very good. But other people do not automatically believe in rebirth and karma. They think that the Dharma is good and helpful, but they have doubt about future lives. They wonder whether karma, cause, and result are really true. This just naturally happens; we can't blame them for it. However, it is important for us to have faith in karma, cause, and result because that faith is the root of our future happiness. Just about everyone in the world is sometimes very happy and sometimes suffers terribly. Why is this? Many people wonder whether this just happens at random without any cause or whether some sort of god or deity makes it so. But it is not either of these. What causes our happiness or suffering is our previous actions. From doing good actions, we accumulate good karma and experience the resulting happiness. Similarly, from doing bad actions and accumulating bad karma, suffering results. This is the fundamental point of the Buddha's teachings, so it is very important for us to believe it.

We need to understand the presentation of karma. We need to

think about it and develop belief in it, but in and of itself, karma can be difficult to grasp. When the Buddha taught the Dharma, he taught that some things are gross phenomena that we can perceive directly. There are also some things that we may not be able to perceive directly, but that we can deduce through inference. But karma, cause, and effect are extremely subtle; we develop faith in them through the words of the Buddha. We cannot see it directly, and we cannot really infer it logically. We need to develop certainty through faith and belief. This is why it is called extremely subtle, which makes it very difficult to perceive. However, if we carefully examine the teachings on karma explained in the abhidharma, we can really develop belief in karma.

It might seem hard to understand karma. But if we look at it, the teachings on karma simply say that if we have a good intention and do a good act, it will bring a good result. If we have a bad intention and do something bad, that will only bring a bad result—harm to ourselves and others. If you actually think about it, it is not all that difficult.

DIFFERENT WAYS TO LOOK AT KARMA AND RESULTS

When the Buddha taught about karma, he said that when we perform an action, it leads to a result. There are many different ways of thinking about karma. We can classify it according to when the result occurs or according to whether it propels a new rebirth or if it ripens during our lifetime. Alternatively, we can consider the manner in which the result occurs or the relationship between the intention and the action. These are a few of the different ways that karma can be categorized.

Classifying Karma by When the Result Is Experienced

If we think about karma in terms of when we experience the result, in general we can say that there are four types. The first is karma that is visibly experienced—that is, experienced in this life. The second is karma that is experienced upon birth—that is, in our next lifetime. The third is karma that is experienced in other lifetimes, and the fourth is karma that is not definitely experienced—that is, karma that may or may not be experienced in some future lifetime, depending upon circumstances. Our virtuous acts fall into these four categories, as do our misdeeds. The reason why there are many different types of karma is that our motivations and actions can be of different strengths. Whether our motivation is virtuous or unvirtuous, sometimes it is strong and sometimes it is weak. Sometimes the act itself is very forceful and powerful; sometimes the act, whether virtue or misdeed, is small. Because of this, there are many different types of karma.

Some of our acts are what we call karma that is visibly experienced: the act and the motivation are so strong that the result comes in this very life. If we do something extremely good and virtuous in this life, its result might be happiness in this very life. There are also instances where someone with a harmful intent does something so extremely negative and harmful that its result happens as sufferings, difficulties, and obstacles in this life. When the motivation is strong and the act is also strong, then the karma will ripen in this lifetime as visibly experienced karma.

Sometimes we perform actions that are not quite so strong, and so they do not ripen in this life but in the next lifetime after we take a new body. This is karma that is experienced upon birth: an action performed in one lifetime whose result ripens in the next. When you see people who are naturally happy and for whom everything always goes well, often this is the result of good acts in their last life. When you see people who are naturally unhappy and for whom everything is difficult, this is often the result of negative and harmful acts in their last lifetime. These would thus be the results of karma experienced upon birth.

The third type of karma is karma experienced in other lifetimes. This is when the motivation is not strong and the act does not do such great help or harm. It is not such a great virtue or wrongdoing. Such acts do not ripen in this life or in the next, but if the right conditions come together in the future, they will ripen then.

Sometimes we perform actions that are quite weak—the act is weak and the motivation is weak. Because this karma is so weak, it is possible that it will not be experienced. A weak virtue might be overpowered by a stronger nonvirtue, or a weak misdeed might be overpowered by a strong virtue. For example, if we commit an action but later regret and confess it sincerely, the karma will not ripen on us, but if we do not feel regret and do not purify it, then when the right conditions come together, the karma will ripen. This is what we call karma that is not definitely experienced.

Propelling Karma and Completing Karma

Another way to explain karma in terms of the manner in which the result is experienced is to say that there are two types of karma: propelling karma and completing karma. Propelling karma is the karma that propels us to take birth in a particular body. Some beings take birth as humans, some as animals, and so forth. The act that makes us take birth as a human or an animal is our propelling karma. For example, as the result of performing a virtuous action, we might take a good birth such as a human birth. The act that initially causes us to take a human birth is a virtuous propelling karma. When the action that propels us to take birth is unvirtuous, it causes us to take a bad rebirth. An action that would cause rebirth as an animal, for example, would be an unvirtuous propelling karma.

In this way, the different types of propelling karmas cause us to take various kinds of births, but once we have taken birth, there are many different ways that we can be. When born as humans, some people lead happy and wonderful lives, whereas some experience great problems and suffering. A being might be born as an animal but have all the food it needs, be comfortable, and lead a relaxed and good life. Other animals experience great suffering—constant hunger, thirst, fear, or other forms of suffering. In both instances, this is because the completing karma—the karma that affects how a being's life proceeds after taking birth—is different.

In this way, the propelling and completing karmas are not necessarily the same. You might have virtuous propelling karma but unvirtuous completing karma. For example, you might have virtuous propelling karma and be born as a human, but because of unvirtuous completing karma you might experience a lot of poverty, illness, and numerous difficulties in your life. Similarly, a being might have an unvirtuous propelling karma that causes birth as an animal, for example, but that animal might have everything it needs—food, drink, nothing to fear, and no problems. This is because its completing karma is virtuous. Sometimes both the propelling and completing karmas are virtuous. For example, one might be reborn in a human body or other good birth and then experience all sorts of joys—plenty of food, great happiness, wealth, and luxury. Sometimes both the propelling and completing karmas are unvirtuous, such as when a being is propelled by its propelling karma into an unfortunate birth as an animal that because of unvirtuous completing karma has no opportunity for happiness in its life.

There are many different types of karma that ripen throughout our lives. Sometimes something happens because of visibly experienced karma. Or it might be karma experienced upon birth or experienced in other lifetimes. Or the karma that ripens now might have been not definitely experienced karma. Many of the events in our lifetimes are the ripening of different individual actions, so many different karmas come into play during our lives. Our lifetime is the result of many different actions. We may have happy times during one period and hard times during another. We may be happy for years during which everything goes well, but then things turn sour for a few years. This is the result of different types of karma—some from acts committed in this life, some from previous lives. Even a hereditary medical condition or mental illness can result from karma. While the illness might have been inherited from your parents, it was the power of your karma to take birth with that particular set of parents, and in this way it comes out of the power of karma.

Similar Experiences and Similar Deeds

When we talk about karma from the Buddhist perspective, there are two different aspects that we need to distinguish: prior karma and the circumstantial conditions. Karma is the main thing, but circumstantial conditions can contribute to the results experienced. For instance, sometimes you get sick because of karma, but sometimes it is because of external circumstances. Sometimes the cause is karma, but the circumstances are contributing factors. Different circumstances can lead to various types of happiness or suffering.

But how do the results happen? In terms of karma, there are two different ways we can experience the result: as the results of similar experiences and as the results of similar deeds. The results of similar experiences occur when, for example, we have a bad intention and perform bad action—harming others. This will lead to a bad result in the future. Or you might have a good and kind intention and do something good, which brings a good result. This is the first way in which karma is experienced, as a similar experience.

The second way is as a similar deed. What this means is that when you have a bad intention and do something bad, you habituate yourself to doing bad things. Then in the future, it is easier to have that bad intention and do that bad thing again. Your intentions get worse and worse; your actions get worse and worse. Then at some point you think, "Wait a minute! This is not good. I'm not going to let myself do anything bad. I want to have good intentions. I want to train myself to do good things." Then you develop good and kind intentions. As a result, you get used to doing good actions, and it just gets better and better. This is a result of similar deeds from getting used to something. If we think about it, we can really see how this happens in the way we develop habits.

Intentions and Acts

If we look at karma in detail, we have to distinguish between our intention and the deed. The intention is mental, and the deed is the act that we perform with our body or speech. These two do not have to be similar, so there are four different possibilities. The first possibility is that we might have a white intention but do a black deed. This means that we have a good, positive intention, but do something bad. The second possibility is to have a black intention and do a white deed. This means that we have a negative, bad intention, and yet do something that seems positive. Or we can have a white intention and do a white deed, where we do something good with a kind intention. The fourth possibility is to have a black intention and do a black deed, where the intention and the deed are both negative.

Of the four possibilities, which do we need? It is very important to have a white intention and perform white deeds. If we can do that, it is best. But the second best is to have a white intention and do black deeds. The deed may not be all that great, but the intention was good, so it is second best. These are the two types of karma that we need. The other two need to be given up. If we have a black intention and do a white deed, because the intention is bad, the act will not bring much benefit. It is likewise important to give up actions where both the intention and the deed are black. Understanding that we must give these up will be helpful for us.

An example of a white motivation and a black deed would be parents who love their children but speak harshly to them when they misbehave. Their motivation is the positive motivation to help their children, but their speech is harsh. Or sometimes we initially have the motivation to do something good, but we might be unable to resist a situation and end up saying something harsh or doing some other negative act. Another example comes from the Jataka tales of the previous lives of the Buddha, which tell of the lifetime when the Buddha was born as Captain Great Courage. He was sailing a ship with five hundred merchants to the islands of jewels, but there was one person on the boat, Black Spearman, who had the evil intention to kill all five hundred merchants, even if he should die in the process. He went into the hold and began to bore a hole in the hull to sink the ship. Captain Great Courage saw what was happening and realized that not only would Black Spearman kill all five hundred merchants, he would also end up going to hell, so Captain Great Courage split his head with an axe and killed him. His motivation was good, but the deed—killing someone—was black.

When we say that the motivation is white, that means that it is a pure motivation. If it is not all that pure, then it becomes a black motivation. We might think we have a pure motivation to help ourselves and others, but we might be mistaken about it and end up doing something harmful. For that reason we really need to examine our motivations extremely carefully. If our motivation is truly white, our acts can lead to vast benefit for a lot of people, but if we are confused and it is really just a black action and a black motivation, that is something that we need to give up. Therefore, we need to analyze whether we have good or bad intentions and whether our actions are good or bad. Our acts will result in either help or harm to both ourselves and others. For this reason, Khenpo Gangshar says:

> It is an unfailing fact that happiness results from virtuous action and that suffering results from having committed unvirtuous karmic deeds.

If you look at how we get habituated to actions, you can see that this is how it really happens.

This is like the root of the Dharma. All of us—ourselves and others—want to be happy and free of suffering, but sometimes people wonder if this is possible. It is possible: we can be happy if we do good things and take up virtue. The reason for this is that virtuous actions are the cause of happiness. We also want to be free of suffering. How is it that we can be free of suffering? To be free of suffering we need to abandon its cause—misdeeds and nonvirtue. If we give those up, we can free ourselves from suffering. That is why karma is unfailing. For that reason we need to take up virtue and abandon nonvirtue, but our ability to do so depends upon our understanding of karma: it is important that we know what kind of act leads to what kind of result.

Identifying Virtue and Wrongdoing

If we are going to take up virtue and give up wrongdoing, we first need to know what they are. As Khenpo Gangshar says:

> Therefore, you must first recognize what is virtuous and what is evil.

We need to know what virtue is and then take it up and put it into practice. Likewise, if we want to be free of suffering, we need to know its cause—misdeeds and nonvirtue—and give it up. We need to identify what is good and what is wrongdoing, or evil. But what does virtue mean? What is nonvirtue? These do not mean that there is a god who has commanded that you should not do this or that. Neither the Buddha nor anyone else has said that you are not allowed to do something, so if you do it, it is wrong. Instead, it comes down to your own mind. When you look at your mind, you can tell whether your acts are virtuous or unvirtuous. As it is said, if we act out of greed, aversion, or delusion, the act is unvirtuous. If we act out of nongreed, nonhostility, or nondelusion, then it is virtuous. This is something we can look at and see for ourselves. When we act with a kind heart and good motivation, without any greed or lust, without any aggression, and without any delusion, that is virtuous. If, on the other hand, we act with a bad motivation out of the greed that wants only to benefit ourselves, out of the aversion that wants to harm someone else, or out of delusion that does not know what to take up and what to give up, that is unvirtuous.

Happiness results from virtue, and unhappiness from nonvirtue. If we look at how things are, we do not have to prove this logically. We all can see that when someone does something with an altruistic intention, it is beneficial for everyone. If someone does something in a malicious or harmful state of mind, with the wish to cause someone pain, it may seem to be successful in the short term, as if they got what they wanted, but ultimately it leads to unhappiness and misfortune. As it is said:

> Distinguish good and bad intentions
> Instead of following the image of good and bad.

This is what it says here, but it is not just what Khenpo Gangshar says. If we look at things around us, we can see it for ourselves.

Sometimes when we look at things, it seems as if someone might do all sorts of terrible things but enjoy all sorts of happiness, wealth, and so forth. You might wonder how that happens. Sometimes there might be a person who has good intentions, always acts kindly, and only does virtuous things, but they always have problems, difficulties, pain, and hardship. It is possible that this can seem to happen in the short term, but it is not a situation where virtue and wrongdoing fail to produce appropriate results. Such a person's present difficulties are the results of negative acts they committed in the past. It is like when someone is moving away and needs to settle their debts before going: the karma from previous lives is ripening on them now. But this person's good deeds of the present are the cause of future happiness. It is primarily through taking up virtue and abandoning wrongdoing that we bring ourselves happiness in the long term.

In order to identify whether an act is virtuous or a misdeed, we need to determine what is the most important factor in committing it: our body, speech, or mind. As Khenpo Gangshar says:

> In order to do this you must determine which is most important: your body, speech, or mind.

When we perform virtuous actions, sometimes we do them with our body, sometimes with our speech, and sometimes with our mind. Likewise, we commit wrongdoing and nonvirtue with our body, speech, and mind. We act with all three, but we need to determine which of these is primary. Sometimes it might seem like one is more important than the other two, or that another is more important. So we need to determine which of these is most important, but in order to determine that, we actually have to understand what our body, speech, and mind are. When we don't think about it, sometimes these seem to overlap and sometimes they seem distinct, but the Buddha carefully explained in his teachings what our body, speech, and mind are.

> To decide this, you must understand what your body, speech, and mind are.

And so what is the body? What is speech? And what is the mind? Sometimes it seems that identifying our body, speech, and mind should be self-evident and easy. In the old days in Tibet, Dharma was primarily taught to people who had an education and training. But

Khenpo Gangshar started a new way of teaching: he taught to everyone, including those without any education. Here he explains this to make it easy for those who had not studied much Dharma:

> The "body" is your physical body that serves as the support
> for benefit and for harm.

So what is our body? In our Buddhist view, we call everything from the crown of our heads to the soles of our feet the body, with all the flesh, blood, bones, organs, and everything in between. Sometimes we feel pleasure, sometimes we feel happiness, and sometimes we feel like we have been helped in some way. Sometimes we suffer; sometimes we feel hurt or sickness. The support for the experience of pleasure or pain, the physical body made of flesh and blood, is what we mean by the body.

> "Speech" is the making of sounds and talking.

Using the body, we can make vocal sounds: we are able to say kind or unkind words. We can have conversations with people and make other people understand our meaning. That is what we call speech.

> The "mind" is that which can think of and recollect any-
> thing at all—that which feels like or dislike and at every
> moment shows different expressions of joy and sorrow. This
> briefly explains the body, speech, and mind.

The root of both the body and speech comes down to the clear awareness that we call our mind. We often have many different types of thoughts that occur in our minds. Sometimes these thoughts are kind; sometimes they are bad. Sometimes we have good thoughts of love, compassion, or bodhichitta. We can have good and kind motivations. Sometimes we have bad thoughts of greed, aversion, or delusion. The mind is that which can generate any of these. Our mind is always changing—in an instant we might suddenly feel joyous, in another, we might feel unhappy. Because of having so many different thoughts and perceptions in our minds, we feel many instances of joy and displeasure, which we then express in many ways through our body or our speech. All of these are what we call mind.

55

This instruction that we need to identify our body, speech, and mind does not appear in other spiritual instructions. But even though it is not found elsewhere, it is a particularly important instruction for our time. The reason is that today, many people think that our mind is our brain, or that the brain and mind are the same thing. The brain is something that can cause thoughts to happen, but if we examine it, we see that the brain is just matter. The mind is awareness. Their characteristics are dissimilar. The brain functions as a support for thoughts, but that does not mean that it is the mind. For example, if you pinch your arm, the arm is a support for thought even though it is not mind itself. It is the same with the brain. The Dalai Lama gives another example: crying out of a strong feeling of compassion and crying out of grief or sadness are very different in terms of motivation, but the brain activity is the same for both, despite the difference in emotion. If one occurred on the right side of the brain and the other on the left, for example, we could say there is a distinction in the brain, but we do not see any such difference. It is important that we recognize that our mind and brain are different—we should not confuse them. The mind is different from the body and the body is different from the mind. It is easy to see that speech is something different, but it is harder to recognize that body and mind are distinct.

Khenpo Gangshar says this solely for the purposes of knowing distinctly what the body, speech, and mind are. He is not discussing the ultimate nature of the body or the nature of the mind. He is simply saying, "This is what we label as the body. This is what we label as speech. This is what we label as mind." In terms of relative and ultimate truth, this is on the level of relative truth. It is not about the ultimate truth.

Determining What Is Most Important

Once we know what our body, speech, and mind are, what is it that performs virtue, and what performs nonvirtue? It is our body, speech, and mind: all three do both virtue and nonvirtue. We can do both virtuous and unvirtuous actions with our body. We can do both virtuous and unvirtuous actions with our speech. We can do both virtuous and unvirtuous actions with our mind. There are three nonvirtues of the body (taking life, stealing, and sexual misconduct), four of speech (lying, harsh speech, divisive speech, and idle chatter), and three of mind (covetousness, malice, and wrong view). There are likewise three virtues of body, four of speech, and three of mind—the opposites of the nonvirtues. But our acts of body, speech, and mind are not necessarily always virtuous or unvirtuous. There is a third type of action, neutral action, which is neither good nor bad.

Although we can do virtuous, unvirtuous, and neutral acts with our body, speech, and mind, we need to see which of these is really the most important. As Khenpo Gangshar says:

> When you commit a virtuous or evil action, you must ask yourself, "Is the body the main thing? Is speech the primary aspect? Or is the mind most important?"

When we commit acts, whether virtuous or unvirtuous, we do them with our body, speech, or mind. We need to identify which is committing the act, but we also need to determine which is actually most important. Whether you are investigating on your own or responding to questions from a master, you must examine which of the three—body, speech, or mind—is the strongest and most powerful. You must ask yourself, "Is the body most important? Is the speech the primary aspect? Or is the mind the most important?"

> Some people will reply that it is the body, some that it is speech, and some will say that the mind is the primary aspect.

If you look at it superficially, some people answer that the body is the most important. The mind thinks of what to do, but it does not actually do anything. If you think of doing something good, it's not until you actually do it with your body that anything has been done. Similarly, when you have bad or malicious thoughts, the mind is thinking, but that is all it can do—it cannot actually go ahead and do that action—and therefore it cannot be the most important. The body actually performs the actions, and we can see it act. It is the body that causes harm to other people or beings. It is with our bodies that we can help people and protect them from suffering. That is why some people think that among the body, speech, and mind, the body is obviously the most important.

Other people think this is wrong because before you physically do something, you talk about it. Then you make the preparations and then perform the act. If you are going to help someone, first you talk about the nice thing you are going to do, then you prepare for it, and then you do it. Similarly, if you do something harmful, first you talk about it, then you prepare to do it, and finally, you commit the act. This is why it is possible that some people might think speech is more important than our bodies.

Some people say that the mind is the most important because you cannot do anything without thinking of it first. Khenpo Gang-shar says:

> In any case, whoever claims that the body or speech is most important has not really penetrated to the core with their examination.

When you look at it superficially, the body performs the act—the mind just thinks and can't actually do anything—so you might think the body is more important. Similarly, we actually say things with our speech—our mind just thinks but says nothing. But actually, the mind is most important. If you say that the body is most important or that speech is most important, then you have not really gotten down to the heart of the matter.

> It is the mind that is the most important. The reason is that unless your mind intends to do so, your body cannot possibly do anything good or bad. Nor can your voice express anything good or evil. Your mind is therefore the primary factor.

Whatever we do, the body will not commit any action without the mind first thinking of it, and our voice will not say anything unless we mentally decide to say it. This is why the mind is most important: without it, you cannot perform any action either physical or verbal. The one to initiate any action is the mind. Only when the mind thinks of it and decides, "I will do this good act," does the body act. Without the mind thinking of it, the body does nothing virtuous. Similarly, without the mind deciding to do something wrong, the body will not commit any misdeeds. When we have a conversation, it is only when the mind decides to say something nice or something hurtful that we say anything good or bad. If you look at the root of it all, the one who is driving the machine is the mind. For this reason, our body and speech are not as important; the mind is the main thing.

Our happiness and suffering come from virtue and wrongdoing, and virtue and wrongdoing depend upon our minds. This is why the most important thing for us to do is to practice tranquility and insight meditation. We need to develop realization in our minds. Do we need to change our body in some way and then take up virtue and abandon nonvirtue? Do we need to alter our speech in some way? These are not the most important thing. The crux that it all comes down to is our mind. We need to transform our mind. We need to make sure that our mind does not go off in the wrong direction. We need to make sure that it goes in the right direction. The wrong direction is delusion and ignorance, so if we put effort into developing our discernment, intelligence, and mental clarity, our minds will turn out well. This is why among our body, speech, and mind, the mind is most important.

Khenpo Gangshar quotes a great meditation master of the past who also made this same point:

> The mind rules over everything like a king,
> The body is a servant for all good or evil deeds.
>
> In that way your mind is like a king and both your body
> and speech are its servants.

The mind is the one with all the power, like the king or the president. First it gives an order, and then the servants—the body and speech—perform the action. If the king-like mind does not say, "Go do that!" your body and speech will not perform any actions.

In addition to physical and verbal actions, there are also events that occur in our mind. For everything that happens in our mind, there are two aspects: the object we are thinking about and the mind itself. We also need to consider which of these two is most important. As Khenpo Gangshar says:

> For instance, when you get angry at your enemy you must examine whether the primary factor is your mind or the enemy. Similarly, when you feel attached to a friend, examine whether your mind or the friend is the primary factor.

Sometimes we meet someone we do not like, we feel aversion to them and think of them as an enemy. Then we might get angry at them. But when we experience that anger or hatred, what is the primary factor—the enemy or our mind? Similarly, when we feel attached to a friend or relative, we need to examine whether the primary factor is our mind or the friend. We need to look at this carefully.

> Examining in this way, you must acknowledge that although the friend and enemy are the circumstances in which attachment and anger arise, the real cause originates in your own mind. Thus, your mind is most important.

When we look at this, the friend or enemy is a condition or circumstance that provokes anger or attachment, but the actual cause originates within our minds. Therefore the mind is most important.

There was a picture taken of Khenpo Gangshar at the time he gave these instructions which shows him holding a phurba, a three-sided dagger, in his right hand, pointing at his own heart. Why is he holding the phurba like that? Some people think that a phurba has the special power to stop ghosts, demons, and other obstructing spirits, so they keep a phurba on their body. They also think that if they fight an enemy, the phurba will block the enemy's weapon. But that is not the reason why Khenpo Gangshar points the phurba at his heart. Other people might say that a phurba is a powerful weapon that we can use to stab our enemies to prevent them from harming us. But that is not the case either—both of these are wrong. The phurba has three sides as a symbol of the antidotes for three poisons of desire, hatred, and delusion. But the three poisons of the afflictions are not outside of us; they are within us. We do not need to stab something outside with the phurba; we stick it inside ourselves. That is why in the picture he isn't stabbing someone else with the phurba—he is pointing at his own heart.

We might think that acting with our body and speech is good and wonder how it could help to meditate with our minds. We might think this ourselves or hear others say it. This is why this is such an important point. If you take control of your mind and have good thoughts, then your body and speech will naturally also be good. If you have bad thoughts in your mind, the body and speech will naturally go down the path of wrongdoing and harm. It is therefore important to recognize that the root of it all is our mind. This view provides the foundation for the following instructions.

5

THE IMPORTANCE
OF MIND

WE NEED TO PRACTICE VIRTUE when doing the analytic meditation of the pandita. In order to bring ourselves happiness, we need to do virtuous things, whether we want temporary or ultimate happiness. Temporary happiness means the enjoyments of this life—our food, clothing, possessions, and so forth. Ultimate happiness is the ultimate freedom from the suffering of samsara, the complete and perfect state of buddhahood. Bringing ourselves both temporary and ultimate happiness is the purpose for which we need to practice virtue and give up nonvirtue.

But how should we practice virtue? We can do virtuous things with our body, speech, and mind. But among these three different ways of practicing virtue, the primary way is with our mind. The mind is king and the body and speech are its servants. If we take control of our mind and transform it in a virtuous direction, then our body and speech will naturally also go in a virtuous direction. That is why we need to make efforts to transform our mind first and foremost.

We often experience attachment and aversion in our minds. When we experience them, the external objects such as our friends or enemies are conditions that help produce them, but the attachment and aversion actually arise from our own mind. This is why we need to examine which is most important. Is the enemy most important, or is the mind most important? When we think about it it, we see that the mind is what is most important.

The great master Shantideva uses a metaphor to show how we cannot eliminate all external problems, and so need to take care of our minds instead:

> To cover all the earth with sheets of leather —
> Where could such amounts of skin be found?
> But with the leather soles of just my shoes
> It is as though I cover all the earth!

If you are walking barefoot, there are all sorts of stones and thorns and things that will cut your feet. You might therefore think you need to cover everything up with leather so that you will not hurt your feet, but to do this you would need a very big piece of leather. If you want to keep going different places, you would eventually have to cover the entire world with leather. But that is not possible — there is just not enough leather in the world. So instead we can just cover our feet with leather. Doing that is the same as covering the surface of the entire earth with leather: we can walk wherever we want without hurting our feet.

It is the same with external enemies. You might feel hatred for them and decide you must get rid of them. But once you have eliminated them, there is another enemy. If you get rid of them, too, then there will be yet another enemy, and in this way you will have more and more enemies. Eliminating the enemies just does not work. So what should we do? We should eliminate the enemy on the inside — our hatred. If we do this, then our outside problems also will be pacified. Everything will then go smoothly for us. It is the same with the friends for whom we feel strong attachment. The attachment comes from our internal mind. If we do not do anything about it, the attachment for the external object — our friend — will grow stronger and stronger. Then the afflictions of clinging, jealousy, and so forth will get stronger and stronger. But if in our own minds we are free of such attachment, we will not cling so tightly to our friends, and we will not have the difficulties that come from excessive clinging to our friends. This is why the mind is most important.

Transforming the Mind: Relative and Ultimate Methods

We need to transform our minds, and generally there are two basic ways we can do this: transforming our minds through relative methods and through ultimate methods. If we want to use the relative methods, we need to rid our minds of ill will and develop our goodwill. In order to do this, we often train in relative bodhichitta, and in particular, the instructions on the lojong mind training. These instructions will help us develop goodwill and a kind heart toward others. We can use these methods to eliminate our ill will toward others. The main method is to practice the tonglen sending and taking meditation.

> Sending and taking should be practiced alternately. These
> two should ride the breath.

In the visualization of sending and taking, we imagine we are giving away all our happiness and goodness. If we are actually able to give away food, clothing, money, and other material things, that is great. But if we are not, we keep in mind the motivation to give our possessions and our happiness away. We imagine giving our happiness to others. At the same time, we visualize taking their suffering away from them and upon ourselves. We generate strong love and compassion, and think to ourselves, "I'm taking away their suffering." We meditate upon giving our happiness away and taking others' suffering. Our meditation follows our breath—giving away our happiness on the exhalation, and taking others' suffering on the inhalation. This method helps us to develop a kind heart, and that in turn eventually helps us to develop bodhichitta. By developing bodhichitta, we will eventually be able to reach the state of perfect benefit for all sentient beings—buddhahood.

There are many similar techniques included within the teachings on mind training. These are wonderful and helpful instructions for helping other beings and ourselves, for quelling our afflictions. But they are not included within Khenpo Gangshar's instructions. He did not teach relative methods; he primarily taught the ultimate methods for transforming our minds. Within these ultimate methods, the main thing we need to do is tame our mind.

> Once you master you own mind, neither friend nor enemy
> will be able to benefit you or cause you harm.

If we have control of our mind, when a condition such as an enemy appears, we will not feel anger, so there will naturally be no harm to ourselves or others. Similarly, when we see a friend or someone we feel affection for, we will not feel attachment and so we will not be harmed in any way. If we do not gain control over our minds, we will be powerless. The reason we meditate is that it is not the external object that is important; if we can transform our minds, the external object will not have much power over us.

> If you don't gain control over your mind, attachment and
> anger will automatically well up, wherever you go and
> wherever you stay.

If we do not have control over our minds, we will naturally feel attachment or anger wherever we go. No matter how far away we go, we will feel attachment or anger. They will well up automatically.

> You must understand that your mind is the root of all joy
> and sorrow, good and evil, attachment and anger.

Whether we feel joy or sorrow, whether we experience good things or bad, what is most important is our mind. Pleasure, displeasure, attachment, and aversion arise, and when they do, among our body, speech, and mind, the mind is most important. Between the mind and the external object, again it is the mind that is most important. We need to understand this thoroughly.

AVOIDING EXTREMES

When the Buddha taught the Dharma, he said that we must not fall into extremes. There are two types of extremes—extremes of view and extremes of conduct. In terms of the extremes of conduct, the first is to fall to the extreme of sense pleasures. In the first part of his life, the Buddha was born a prince, the son of a great king, and he had all the possessions he could possibly need. But he did not feel any attachment to them, and he gave them up—he renounced his kingdom with all its wealth and enjoyments. The Buddha saw that none of this had any essence, so he gave up all these pleasurable things. This illustrates not falling to the extreme of sense pleasures.

The second extreme to avoid is that of austerities and difficulties. After he left the palace, the Buddha spent six years practicing austerities in the forest. During that time, he took very little food or water—he just practiced. He strove single-mindedly to develop his meditation through austerities and difficulties. He did not wash—he just sat there practicing. Yet he realized after six years that these austerities would not bring him to buddhahood, no matter how hard he practiced them, and so at that point he gave them up. He ate food, drank water, and took a bath, avoiding the extreme of austerities that could not bring him to full awakening.

During the time when he was practicing austerities, the Buddha had a group of disciples who later became known as the Good Group of Five. When the Buddha gave up the austerities, at first they did not understand. They had thought the way he was practicing such austerities was wonderful—he had been so diligent! Then it seemed as if he lost heart and got discouraged. When he started eating again, they were disappointed in him and rebelled. They left him, thinking they would never have anything more to do with him.

It is important that we avoid the extremes of either austerities or sense pleasures. Neither of these will bring us to buddhahood. What will bring us there is to tame our own mind. Then we will be able to develop the samadhi meditation that will bring us to complete and perfect buddhahood. This is what the Buddha realized. After bathing and taking food, he went to Bodhgaya and took his seat beneath the Bodhi Tree. He thought to himself, "I am going to sit here and meditate until I attain complete and perfect awakening." And that is what he did, sitting in deep samadhi until he awakened to complete and perfect buddhahood. Once he had achieved that, he had perfected all the qualities of realization and totally given up everything there was to abandon, realizing the profound, pure, peaceful Dharma. He realized:

> Deep, peace, unelaborate, luminous, noncompound—
> Like nectar it is, this Dharma I've found!
> Whomever I teach it could not understand it,
> And so without speaking I'll stay in this wood.

The Buddha realized the dharma nature just as it is—profound, peaceful, free of elaborations, luminous, and noncompounded, but he also thought that those to whom he taught it would not be able to realize it. It is difficult to find. And so in order to create the perception that Dharma is rare, he sat in perfect samadhi in solitude in the forest for seven weeks, enjoying his wonderful meditation without teaching the Dharma.

While he sat there, in order to create the perception of the greatness of the Dharma, the gods Brahma and Indra came down and supplicated him to teach and turn the wheel of Dharma. The Buddha agreed, and he asked himself to whom he should first teach the Dharma. As he sat in samadhi, he looked within his meditation and saw the Good Group of Five who had rebelled against him a few weeks earlier. He thought he should teach the Dharma to them. Since they were in Varanasi, he went there to turn the wheel of Dharma for them.

Now at that point the Good Group of Five had decided among themselves that they would have nothing to do with Siddhartha. At first he had been a prince, but he could not manage that. Later he tried austerities, but he could not handle that either. He couldn't handle anything, they thought, so they agreed that none of them should say a single word to him or listen to a single thing that he said. They would not even acknowledge his presence—they would just sit and ignore him.

But when the Buddha arrived, he was glorious! He was so majestic that first one got up and knelt before him, and then a second, and a third, and soon they were all kneeling on their right knee, their left knee raised and hands joined in prayer at their hearts. It was the magnificence of the Buddha that made it possible for them to come back to him, and then he turned the wheel of the Dharma for them.

Which wheel of Dharma did the Buddha turn first? The Buddha realized that he had to teach the Dharma progressively, and so first he taught the relative truth, then the ultimate truth, and then the instructions on how to attain the ultimate result. Thus he taught the three wheels of the foundation vehicle, the great vehicle, and the secret mantra vajrayana, in that order.

THE FIRST WHEEL
Selflessness and the Foundation Vehicle

When the Buddha turned the wheel of Dharma of the foundation vehicle, he primarily taught the four noble truths. Basically, the four noble truths come down to the selflessness of the individual. The teaching of the selflessness of the individual is important because we experience all sorts of suffering in samsara, and the root of all of this is karma. Where does karma come from? Karma results from our afflictions, primarily the three poisons of desire, aversion, and delusion. When we see something attractive, we feel desire for it. When we see something we don't want, we feel aversion toward it. This causes us to act and accumulate karma.

Therefore we need to get rid of these afflictions, but how do we do that? If we simply think to ourselves that we will never again feel desire, aversion, or delusion, will that get rid of them? It will not— we cannot just stop our desire, aversion, or delusion, because they happen automatically. We have been habituated to them since beginningless time, and so they arise naturally.

We need to get rid of them, but how? We cannot eliminate them directly, but we can do it indirectly by giving up their cause. That cause is clinging to a self. We think, "Me!" and cling to a sense of "me." We think, "I want something good," and then feel desire for it. When we think "That's going to hurt me," we feel aversion or hatred. When we do not understand the nature of the self, then we experience delusion. It is this thinking "me" and clinging to an individual self that we need to eliminate.

Can we just think to ourselves that we will not cling to a self anymore? Will that work? It will not, because from beginningless time until now, we have had the habit of clinging to "me" and "mine." We cannot just say we won't do that anymore, but that does not mean we cannot get rid of it. We can look to see what ego-clinging is rooted in. If we can pull it out from its roots, then we will also get rid of the branches.

What is clinging to a self rooted in? Actually, it is not rooted in anything. If we see that, then naturally ego-clinging will not happen. The reason it has no root is that when we look for the object that we are clinging to as "me," as a self, we cannot find it.

When we talk about clinging to a self, often we talk about clinging to "me" or clinging to "mine." We think, "Oh, this is me" and we cling to whatever that is. Or we think, "I want that thing. This is mine." But when we really look at what this "me" is, where is it? We cannot really find it anywhere. When we see there is really no "me" to cling to, then naturally the thought of clinging to "me" is going to be pacified. Likewise, there can be no "mine." When we cling to a "me" or "mine," then we want things or we feel aversion to them, and this makes all of the afflictions arise. Because of the afflictions, we are stuck in samsara. But if we realize that "me" and "mine" do not really exist at all, then clinging to a "me" and "mine" will naturally be quelled. And if that is quelled, then the afflictions will naturally be pacified. That is why we meditate upon the selflessness of the individual.

In investigating this, if we first think about clinging to "mine" and realize that there is not really any object to cling to, then we will understand that clinging to "mine" is illusory. Then it will be easy to realize that clinging to "me" is also illusory. For instance, if I have a glass of water on the table, I cling to it as being mine. But what is it really? Someone put a glass here and poured water into, so now I say that it is my water, but what is the reason for saying so? There really is no reason. But I cling to it, and if someone came and drank it, then I would get angry—how dare he drink my water! That is how the afflictions arise out of clinging to "mine," but if you examine this situation, what is the connection between me and the water? There is no real connection between the two, so how could it really be mine? But even though there is no connection and there is not any real "mine," we think there is, and thinking that way makes us get angry.

Let's consider an example of how clinging to "me" and "mine" creates suffering. If we were to go into a store and a watch that was for sale fell on the floor and broke, we would not think much of it. But if we were to drop our own watch and it broke, we would feel upset. If the mechanism broke and it stopped, we would be unhappy. If we look to see what this comes from, it comes from saying the watch is "mine." But where is the "mine"? If we look for it, we will not find it inside the watch, or outside, or between the outside and inside. Actually, there is not much difference between the watch in the store and our own watch, but because we cling to one as "mine," we experience feelings of suffering. If there were no thought of "mine," there would be no suffering. If we examine our clinging to objects and see that there really is no "mine," and we realize egolessness, this is very beneficial.

Similarly, when we think about our body and mind we often think "my body" or "my mind." But sometimes we think "the body is me" or "the mind is me." Sometimes we think of them as being "me" and sometimes as something that we possess. When we think, "This is my mind," it is as if "me" is something other than mind. Or we think, "This is my body," as if the "me" were again something other than the body. Sometimes the body and mind are "me," sometimes they are "mine," and in the end we cannot be certain what "me" is. If we look for it in this way, we are unable to find anything that we definitely know to be the self.

When we realize that there really is no self, then we can meditate on that. First we study it and develop certainty in it. Then we can meditate on it and actually realize the selflessness of the individual. When we realize that, we can eliminate all of the afflictions. When they have been eliminated, we will stop performing karmic actions, will no longer wander in samsara, and we will achieve the status of an arhat. Thus, this is the way to tame our own minds—the method taught in the foundation vehicle for realizing the selflessness of the individual.

THE SECOND WHEEL
Emptiness and the Great Vehicle

The second time the Buddha turned the wheel of Dharma, he gave the teachings of the great vehicle or mahayana about the emptiness of all phenomena. These are the teachings on transcendent intelligence, which primarily teach that all phenomena are empty and self-less. Thus there are two types of selflessness: the selflessness of the individual and the selflessness of phenomena.

In the mahayana, there is the tradition of the middle-way school. Whether we are discussing the view of the self-empty or other-empty schools, the middle way proposes that we need to abandon the afflictions, which are the root of everything. If we can do so, we will be able to abandon the suffering of samsara. The method by which we can abandon the afflictions is to meditate on the essence of all phenomena and realize that it is emptiness. Everything that appears to us is just a confused perception. All phenomena are like dreams and illusions. By meditating on the selflessness of phenomena in addition to the selflessness of the individual, we can understand this dreamlike or illusory nature of everything we perceive. Then when suffering occurs, it does not harm us. You may dream of something, but when you wake up it is not there and you are freed from any pain or suffering that the confused perception of it produced. This is why we need to realize emptiness. If when afflictions arise, we know that they do not inherently exist and we meditate on that and see the nature of emptiness as it is, we can attain the ultimate result.

The method taught in the middle-way school to realize the emptiness of all phenomena is to carefully consider and contemplate the reasoning that leads to this conclusion. Therefore in the middle way one examines phenomena and tries to see what they are like. How do they arise? After they have arisen, how do they stay? Then how do they cease? We examine this in great detail with extremely subtle reasoning, including the logic that examines causes, essence, and so forth. We can follow this logic and develop an understanding and definite recognition that everything is emptiness. If we meditate on this, we no longer experience any fear, pain, or attachment from our confused perceptions and we realize they are emptiness.

Within the middle way there are different ways of doing this. In the tradition of the self-empty school, we first come to understand the emptiness of all phenomena. By seeing and understanding this, we can rid ourselves of confused perceptions. In the approach of the other-empty school, we meditate not only on the emptiness of all phenomena, but that the essence of this emptiness is all the qualities—it is buddha nature. But in both the self-empty and the other-empty school, we are primarily examining reality with logic and reasoning. After contemplating the reasons, we develop the understanding that this is how things are and then meditate on that.

At the root of everything are the afflictions; as a result of the afflictions we see all the confused appearances of samsara. But these confused appearances do not inherently exist, and so the Buddha used examples to show that they are empty. First we think about coarse outer objects. Such objects, if they really exist, must be either single or multiple. But when we look for a single thing, we cannot find it because coarse outer objects are actually made up of multiple atoms all grouped together. All of the external things we can see are nothing more than an agglomeration of tiny particles—there is nothing else there. For instance, if we have a pile of dirt we can call it a pile, but actually it is just a bunch of dirt that happens to be heaped up together. We think that there is one solid thing but actually, if we examine it, it is all these other little things all brought together. That is why you cannot really say that coarse outer things have any reality—you cannot find the real coarse thing there. You can prove through logic that coarse things are all collections of particles.

Then when we think about particles, they are really nothing other than just something that appears to our mind. In reality, they do not inherently exist—we cannot find them. This is what the Buddha taught, and later masters have explained it in the treatises. In modern physics (although I do not know the subject well), they also say that particles cannot be established—they are just capacity or energy coming together, but actually there is no real thing there. These teachings—the teachings of the Buddha, the teachings in the treatises, and the views of the scientists—are essentially the same: they all say that coarse phenomena cannot be truly established. When we realize this, we see that all phenomena are empty. When we see that, we realize that the objects toward which we feel attachment or aversion do not have any real existence of their own. Thus, by realizing emptiness we are able to realize the nature of all phenomena.

This is how we examine external things logically and come to know what they are like. We can then meditate on this and thus really come to understand and know that they are empty.

Our mind is similar, but instead of thinking in terms of particles, we can think about it in terms of time—years, months, days, or hours. Our mind is changing each and every moment. Can any given moment be established as anything? Some people say that there is a finite, indivisible moment of time, but such a moment cannot be proven to actually exist and thus must also be emptiness.

In this way, external objects are empty and the internal mind does not inherently exist. We can contemplate this and come to know it. Then we can meditate on it. But our meditation needs a helper, and the helper that it needs is the six transcendences. The most important helper is transcendent intelligence, which is realizing the dharma nature just as it is. This is not just blind faith. It is a question of examining it, understanding it, and really developing true conviction. Then when you have this conviction, you meditate upon it. Through meditation you gain a clearer and clearer perception of it. That clear perception of the nature of things is transcendent intelligence, prajñāpāramitā. As a helper to develop that, we need the other five transcendences: transcendent generosity, discipline, patience, diligence, and meditation. These are the helpers which help us develop wisdom so that we can achieve the ultimate result of buddhahood. This is the path taught by the great vehicle.

THE THIRD WHEEL
Buddha Nature and the Vajrayana

If the emptiness of all phenomena were blank nothingness, it would be inanimate, material emptiness. With humans, for instance, if the body has clear awareness, it is a person, but if there is no clear mind, it is just a corpse. It is similar with emptiness. There is emptiness that has clarity and emptiness that lacks clarity. If emptiness has no clarity at all, then it is inanimate emptiness, such as, for example, the void of space. Nothing bad can happen to it, but no qualities can arise within it, either. It does not have any potential; it is inert.

Is the empty nature like that? It is not. The emptiness of all phenomena has clarity and the aspect of clear wisdom. It has the clarity that during the pure phase has the potential to arise as the wisdom of a buddha and during the impure phase can arise as all the impure appearances of interdependence. Emptiness and this clarity are unified. When we do not recognize this, we are confused, but if we recognize it, it is the potential or seed for achieving all the qualities of buddhahood. This is present within all sentient beings; it is buddha nature.

Thus in the first wheel of Dharma, the Buddha taught the selflessness of the individual. In the second wheel of Dharma, he taught emptiness. And in the third wheel of Dharma, he taught that emptiness is one with clear wisdom, that the cause of buddhahood is present within the mind streams of all beings. The actual thing we meditate on—the root of our practice—is emptiness, but not inanimate emptiness like space. It has the potential for the Buddha's wisdom to arise. Buddhas have wisdom, love, and power. The seed for this wisdom, love, and power is present in emptiness. This emptiness permeates us all. This is the meaning of the third wheel of Dharma.

These teachings of the foundation and great vehicles were brought to Tibet, but when we practice Tibetan Buddhism, do we actually meditate on the view of selflessness from the foundation vehicle? Actually, no, we do not really meditate on it that much. Do we follow the methods of meditating on emptiness from the mahayana? Well, actually we do not spend a whole lot of time meditating on that, either. We primarily meditate upon the instructions of the secret mantra vajrayana.

However, when we are studying, we try to fully comprehend the foundation-vehicle view of the lack of an individual self and the great-vehicle view of emptiness. You might think it is just some sort of mere intellectual exercise—we are just thinking for thinking's sake. But that's not really what it is. This is actually a way of coming to understand how things are. Then when we come to practicing the instructions from the secret mantra vajrayana on the nature of the mind, we are able to have real certainty in them. We're able to really believe them fully. This is why when we practice the Dharma in the Tibetan tradition, first we study the views of the foundation and great vehicles thoroughly. Through this we develop certainty so that when we come to a critical point in our practice we will realize, "That's what that is!" This is why studying is very helpful for our meditation.

The Path of Means and the Path of Liberation

Within the instructions of the secret mantra vajrayana, there are two different types of paths that we can practice: the path of means and the path of liberation. The path of means includes the practices of the creation stage, which consists in visualizing ourselves as a yidam deity or visualizing the deity before us. There are many different types of creation-stage practices we can do: the practices of Vajrasattva, Manjushri, Tara, Vajravarahi, Guru Rinpoche, and so forth. This is meditation on the body of a deity. Although creation-stage meditation is not taught in these instructions, if you practice it, it will be very helpful. But it is part of the path of means and is not included here.

Sometimes we also visualize the deity's body dissolving into the absence of a focus—emptiness. That is a practice of the completion stage. There are actually two different types of completion-stage practices: those with attributes and those without attributes. Completion-stage practices with attributes are practices such as tummo, dream yoga, or various other methods—there are many different methods for completion-stage practices. These are all part of the path of means.

The path of liberation is just getting right down to meditation. When we meditate on the path of liberation, all phenomena are empty, and we first establish a full understanding of the selflessness of the individual and of dharmas. But if we were to meditate upon outside objects, we would be using logic to generate belief and confidence in emptiness. We could say, "Yes, that's really what it is like." But it is difficult for such meditation to lead to an actual experience of emptiness. That is why in the sutra practices of the great vehicle we talk about gathering merit through the practices of the six transcendences and why it takes a long time—uncountable aeons—to achieve the ultimate result.

But the practices of the secret mantra vajrayana do not take an uncountable number of aeons. In the best of circumstances, we can do these practices and attain complete buddhahood in one lifetime and one body. If we cannot do it in one lifetime, then we can do it in perhaps three, seven, or sixteen lifetimes. We will be able to attain buddhahood in that period, which is why this is called the fast path. What is the special feature of the fast path? Although we recognize that external objects are empty, we do not pay much attention to them. Instead, the root of what we do is to just look at the nature of the mind. Why do we do that? Although external things are empty, when they appear to us we do not see that they are just a projection of our inner mind; we do not see that they are empty. They seem solid. We can think that solid-seeming things are empty all we want, but it is very difficult to actually realize this.

It is different if we look at our own mind. Before we examine the mind, we have many different thoughts and motivations—the mind can think up anything at all. As we discussed above, the mind is like a powerful king who rules over everything. But if we look at the nature of that which is exercising power, we see that it cannot be established as anything. We can't say it stays here, it goes there, it is over there,. There's nothing definite there. It is as if it were some false thing that appears. But if we look at the essence of that appearance, it is easy to see that the essence of the mind is emptiness. If we think about it, it is easy to understand that the mind is empty, and if we look at the nature of mind, it is actually relatively easy to have an experience of emptiness of the mind. If we look at external things like houses, mountains, forests, or what have you, it is very difficult to come to an experience of emptiness. We might think, "Oh, that's empty," but immediately having some sort of experience of that emptiness is really very difficult. That is why we look at the nature of the mind.

When we look at the nature of the mind, we can use inference, or instead we can use direct perception: we can experience this through the wisdom of self-awareness. We can actually come to an experience of the empty nature of the mind. But we see that emptiness is not just some sort of blank, inanimate void. Rather, emptiness has a clear aspect and the capacity to appear as anything. It is not like the emptiness of space. When we talk about how things can be empty, there are, in general, two different ways that things can be empty. Something can be empty like empty space, but that emptiness cannot really do anything for us. It does not help us in any way; it cannot really bring us anything. The emptiness of the nature of mind is not like that. Whether we call it the nature of mind or the dharma nature, this emptiness can develop into all the various qualities of a buddha. It is empty but knowing at the same time. A simple way to explain this is to call it the union of clarity and emptiness. The mind is empty, but at the same time it is clear and knowing; that clarity is also empty. These two are brought together and unified.

If we look at it on a more profound level, we would call this the union of the expanse and wisdom. Expanse means the dharma expanse—the expanse of the nature of all phenomena that is naturally empty, the dharmadhātu. Wisdom refers to the clear wisdom that arises. The essence of that clear wisdom is emptiness, but this emptiness is not blank and inanimate. The practice of the secret mantra is to experience this and meditate upon it.

6

APPEARANCES
AND MIND

T HE KEY POINT IS THAT the mind is primary, but we can take
control over it. It is easy to do so. It is easy to realize its nature,
and so we are extremely fortunate. This is why in vajrayana practices
in general, and in mahamudra and dzogchen in particular, we put
emphasis on the mind and meditate on it. When Khenpo Gangshar
teaches that the mind is most important, the source for this instruction is Longchen Rabjam, a great master who was a contemporary
of the Third Karmapa Rangjung Dorje. Khenpo Gangshar cites two
passages from Longchenpa. The first passage reads:

> The Great Omniscient One has said:
>
> > When under the influence of dhatura,
> > All the various experiences you have, whatever they
> >   may be,
> > Are all, in fact, mistaken images without existence.
> > Likewise, understand that under the influence of a
> >   confused mind
> > All the mistaken experiences of the six classes of beings,
> >   whatever they may be,
> > Are all empty images, nonexistent yet appearing.

The Great Omniscient One is an epithet for Longchen Rabjam. He wrote a great number of extensive and helpful treatises, the most profound of which are collected in a text called *The Seven Treasuries of Longchenpa*. What Longchenpa said, in describing how things appear to us, is that various things appear to us, but even though they appear, they are not inherently real. This is what we call emptiness in the treatises on transcendent intelligence and the middle way. Although things do not truly exist, they appear solid in our confused, relative perception. The reason they are confused appearances is that they are like the hallucinations one sees after taking dhatura, a hallucinogenic plant also called thorn apple. When you take dhatura, you see different colors and shapes or hear many different sounds. You might feel ecstatic, or you might feel very depressed. But all of the experiences that you have while high on this hallucinogen are in fact mistaken images. They are not really there. They appear to you, but they do not exist in any way. This is the analogy.

The meaning of the analogy is that it is the same with us now. Just as if we had taken a hallucinogen, whatever happy or sad appearances we see are samsaric, confused appearances of the mind. Even when we are not intoxicated, everything we perceive in this life comes out of the confusion that arises from the power of karma. Whether we have the perception of being human or animal, whether we perceive the appearances of earth, water, fire, or air, whatever appearances we see come out of the power of a mistaken mind. All the external forms we see or sounds we hear are just emptiness. Whatever appears internally within our mind is also just emptiness—none of it is actually there. Thus all of the different experiences of the six classes of beings, whatever they may be, are empty images, nonexistent yet appearing. Longchenpa and Khenpo Gangshar are saying the same thing: the mind is the root of everything.

This passage teaches that all appearances are our mind—they arise within our mind and they cannot be established outside of ourselves. Because of this, we need to follow the instruction given in the second quotation from Longchenpa:

> Since they appear in your mind and are constructed by
>   your mind,
> Exert yourself in taming this mistaken mind.

External appearances appear to the mind, but they are just a construction of the mind—when they appear, the mind gives them a label. For that reason, even if outside things seem good, there is not actually a whole lot to be attached to. If they seem bad, there is nothing to feel aversion toward. Therefore if we want to be free of suffering and faults and find happiness and good qualities, the most important thing is to tame our mind and to be diligent about doing so. This is why we meditate, and this is why there are mind instructions. Since the mind is the root of everything and everything comes down to the mind, there is nothing more important than taming our mind, meditating on samadhi, and resting in equipoise.

The first passage says that appearances are mind; they are not separate from mind. The second passage says that we need to thoroughly tame our own mind. These are Longchenpa's instructions. Next, Khenpo Gangshar gives his own advice:

> But you shouldn't take your understanding from books or
> stories heard from others. Recognize, yourself, that appearance is mind and understand that your mind is the root of
> all phenomena.

We must not take all of our understanding from what we read. If we have understanding from a book, we will think the book says such and such so it is probably something like that. You read something in a book and then think, "Oh, that's how it probably is." Maybe you have studied the logic of the mind-only school and think, "It's all mind. Everything that appears is mind." This is just a conceptual understanding, and it is not all that helpful. You might hear someone say something like this, and think, "So-and-so said they're all just appearances in the mind, so it must be like that." On one level we know it; it is okay. But it is really not enough. What we need is not a conceptual understanding that comes from study and reasoning; we actually need to have the experience of it.

THREE WAYS OF KNOWING

There are three ways in which we can know something. We can have understanding, we can have experience, or we can have realization. Understanding is when you think about something through inference. Your mind is directed outward and you think, "Oh, it is probably like that." Is that understanding good? Of course it is, but it does not have the power to help us develop the ultimate qualities that we really need. So it is not enough. It is not enough because it is not an internal meditation. Instead, it is turning the mind outward and thinking about external things. This is what is meant here by understanding, and it is not what we need.

You might also know something through hearsay or stories. You might have heard someone say that is how it is — "They say that appearances are all mind." You might think some great lama or great scholar said so. "There's this great mahasiddha who taught this and that's probably how it is." But that is not what we need; that is also just mere understanding. Of course learning things through reading and listening to teachers is good, but it can't really produce realization. This is why we should not rely solely on what we read in books or on hearsay.

We need to experience and realize the nature of the mind for ourselves. Experience comes when we are meditating and we think to ourselves, "This is what the mind is like!" But this is not stable at first. We need to meditate on it and cultivate that experience, and eventually it will become stable, which is what we call realization. We need to turn our mind inward to look at itself. We can recognize for ourselves that appearance is mind and that the mind is the root of all phenomena, both external appearances and all our afflictions. This is recognizing that appearances are mind. We need to know this, but it should not just be an understanding. We cannot just leave it as something we heard from someone; we need to develop an experience of it within our own minds.

THE MAHAMUDRA PRESENTATION
Mind, Appearances, and Coemergence

In the instructions of mahamudra, this is called recognizing that appearances are mind. In the mahamudra teachings, the Ninth

Karmapa Wangchuk Dorje explains this in his book *Pointing Out the Dharmakaya*. The book has ten chapters on insight meditation, five of which are about the view and five about pointing out. One of the five chapters about the view presents the view that appearances are mind, and one of the five chapters on pointing out is called "Pointing out that appearances are mind." These chapters present essentially the same teaching as Khenpo Gangshar does here. Wangchuk Dorje also gives essentially the same instructions in *Eliminating the Darkness of Ignorance*, but in his longer treatise, *Mahamudra: The Ocean of Certainty*, he presents the instructions a little bit differently. He treats looking at the mind in stillness and looking at the mind in motion very briefly, and then discusses recognizing appearances as mind much more extensively. He presents four points: appearances are mind, mind is empty, emptiness is spontaneous presence, and spontaneous presence is naturally liberated. The words are different, but the meaning is basically the same.

The fifteenth-century master Takpo Tashi Namgyal also wrote two books of mahamudra instructions. The longer work is called *Moonbeams of Mahamudra*, and the shorter is called *Clarifying the Natural State*. Both of these treatises make essentially the same point, although it is a bit more detailed in *Moonbeams of Mahamudra* and briefer in *Clarifying the Natural State*. These texts use three terms—coemergent mind-essence, coemergent appearance, and coemergent thoughts—which were also used by Lord Gampopa.

Coemergent mind-essence means looking at the nature of the mind and seeing that it is coemergent. This is not a question of whether or not we realize the nature of mind. The essence of the mind occurs at the same time as mind, and the presence of the mind-essence in that very moment is what we call the coemergent mind-essence. When we see that the mind-essence is coemergent, this means that we know the nature of the mind fully and thoroughly.

Because we really know the nature of the mind and its coemergent essence, we see that appearances are coemergent with it—they arise at the same time as the nature of the mind. There is nothing new that happens when we recognize the nature of appearances. This means that appearances are naturally the same as the essence of the mind: they are also naturally empty of essence. That is coemergent appearance.

When Gampopa taught this, he said, "The coemergent mind-essence is the dharmakaya. Coemergent appearance is the radiance of the dharmakaya." Gampopa had a disciple named Je Gomtsul, who also happened to be his nephew. Je Gomtsul listened to these instructions and added a third line: "Coemergent thought is the energy of the dharmakaya." The movement of all our thoughts is like the power of the dharmakaya. Coemergent thought means that thoughts are not something that we throw away and only then does wisdom occur. The two happen simultaneously.

These are the three types of coemergence taught in both *Moonbeams of Mahamudra* and *Clarifying the Natural State*. What Khenpo Gangshar is teaching here is coemergent appearance—how we need to recognize that appearances are mind.

DISTINGUISHING APPEARANCES AND PERCEIVED OBJECTS

In general, all appearances are mind, but when beginners meditate and receive mind instructions, they easily see that some things are mind but have difficulty seeing other things as mind. This is why in the context of this presentation, Khenpo Gangshar says that we need to differentiate appearances from perceived objects. As the text says:

> In this context, you must distinguish between appearance and the perceived object.

Appearances are all the feelings we have—greed, aversion, love, compassion, guilt, depression, joy, excitement, or anything else. These appear in the mind and anyone can easily see that these are mind. When we say perceived objects, we mean the forms, sounds, smells, and so forth, that are the objects of our senses. These seem like material objects that exist outside of ourselves.

It was Longchen Rabjampa who said that one must distinguish between appearances and perceived objects. Khenpo Gangshar Rinpoche considered this instruction very important. He said that not distinguishing between appearances and perceived objects can create a lot of problems. As the Great Omniscient One, Longchenpa, said:

> Ignorant people claim that everything is mind.
> They are deluded about the three types of appearance,
> Have many shortcomings, mix things up and overexaggerate.
> Meditators, give up such unwholesome ways!

Foolish, ignorant people might claim that everything is mind, but they are totally deluded about the nature of the three types of appearances: appearances, the feelings and experiences we have in our mind; perceived objects, the forms, sounds, scents, tastes, and touches that appear as external objects; and the perceiver, our own mind. If we do not distinguish among these, we will be deluded. Saying that all of these are just mind creates a lot of problems: you will mix everything up or overexaggerate. There are many absurd consequences that arise out of this, so it is not logically tenable. This is why he says give up such unwholesome ways.

For this reason, we must distinguish between perceived objects and appearances. So what are perceived objects? What are appearances? Khenpo Gangshar explains:

> The mere presence of visible forms, sounds, and so forth,
> that are the objects of the six types of consciousness is called
> "perceived objects."

The mere presence of visible forms means that there is the mere appearance of forms before the eye. There are also the appearances of sounds to the ear, there are scents that appear to the nose, there are tastes that appear to the tongue, there are touches that appear to the body, and there are all the dharmas the mind can think of. These are the objects of the six consciousnesses. Each of the different faculties and consciousnesses has its own object, the mere appearance of which is the perceived object: when it seems as if there is a visual form, an audible sound, or another object of the six consciousnesses, that object is what we call the perceived object.

> Thoughts of attachment, anger, or delusion based on the "perceived objects" are "appearances," for example, the feeling of attachment to a pleasant object, the feeling of anger toward an unpleasant one and the indifferent feeling toward something neutral. You must understand that such appearances are the functions of your own mind.

When an object appears, if it is something pleasant, we think it is nice. Then we want it and get attached to it. Or perhaps we see something unpleasant and think it is no good—we do not want it. We feel aversion to it. Sometimes we perceive something that is neither pleasant nor unpleasant. We do not think of it as good, nor do we think of it as bad. We neither like nor dislike it; we just experience indifference or delusion—we do not really know it. These thoughts of attachment, aversion, or delusion that arise based upon the perceived object are what we here call appearances.

But where do these thoughts occur? They occur in our mind—they are not present in the external objects themselves. They are just thoughts, merely a function of the mind. If we put the perceived objects aside for a moment, it is clear that when we dislike something that we have perceived, that is just mind. When happiness occurs, it occurs in the mind. When the affliction of aversion occurs, it occurs in the mind. When anger occurs, it occurs in the mind. The three different types of thoughts—attachment, aversion, and delusion—are not present in external objects; they are in the mind. Whatever various feelings we have arise in the mind. Such thoughts are appearances.

CONSCIOUSNESSES AND THEIR OBJECTS

The Third Karmapa Rangjung Dorje taught that our mind has eight different consciousnesses, of which six engage external objects. These six consciousnesses are either conceptual or nonconceptual. The nonconceptual consciousnesses include the eye consciousness which sees forms; the ear consciousness which hears sounds by engaging audible objects; the nose consciousness which smells scents, whether pleasant or unpleasant; the tongue consciousness which tastes flavors both good and bad; and the body consciousness which feels touches that are soft, rough, and so forth. These five are known as the five consciousnesses of the five gates, as they are supported by the five faculties of the eyes, ears, nose, tongue, and body, and actually engage the external objects of form, sound, scent, taste, and touch. They experience their objects through direct perception.

When we talk about the six consciousnesses, we add the sixth, mental consciousness to these five. The sixth, mental consciousness does not have a material faculty. Our thoughts can think anything at all. Sometimes they follow an eye consciousness automatically, sometimes they follow an ear consciousness, or sometimes they follow a nose consciousness, or another sense consciousness. Thoughts do not engage the external object directly; instead they engage a meaning generality, a conceptual idea of the object in the mind, and think many things, such as "This is good" or "That is bad." This is why the sixth consciousness is considered a conceptual consciousness. Sometimes it experiences excitement, and sometimes it experiences depression. The one who does all these jobs is the conceptual mental consciousness.

In the *Treasure of Valid Logic*, Sakya Pandita writes:

> Sense consciousnesses are like mutes with eyes,
> While thoughts are blind but talkative.
> Self-awareness has all its faculties
> And conveys meaning to the two.

Sense consciousnesses can't really say anything, nor do they know how to think of anything as good or bad. For example, when the eye consciousness sees form, it sees blue, yellow, red, white, or whatever other color, but it does not really have the thought, "This is blue," or "That is white." In contrast, the sixth, mental consciousness is like a loquacious blind person. It does not actually see forms or hear sounds, but it thinks within itself about good, bad, yesterday, or today. When the eye sees something, for example, it can't see yesterday, nor can it see tomorrow. It only sees what is right in front of it today. But the sixth, mental consciousness is different because it can think, "I went there yesterday" or "I'm going to that place tomorrow."

There is no real connection between the nonconceptual consciousnesses such as the eye consciousness and the sixth, mental consciousness. The mute who can see perceives things but cannot say much about them. A blind talker can speak, but cannot see. It does not know what is right in front of it. They are not connected, but there is self-awareness. When we say that the mind is self-aware, this means that we know what we are aware of. Self-awareness knows whatever the eye sees. Self-awareness knows whatever the sixth consciousness is thinking of. Whatever the mute eye consciousness sees works as a sign, which self-awareness knows. It is as if self-awareness goes and talks to the loquacious blind sixth consciousness, and the three work things out. That's how the mind works.

This text discusses only the six consciousnesses, but fundamentally there are eight consciousnesses. The six consciousnesses are unstable consciousness, like waves in the ocean. Sometimes there is an eye consciousness, or sometimes an ear, nose, qr other consciousness. Thoughts occur in the mind; we see forms and hear sounds. Various things occur, but they are changing. The six consciousnesses are changeable.

The stable consciousnesses are said to be the afflicted mind and the all-ground consciousness. When we say "all-ground consciousness," this means the root of all consciousnesses. Whether we are looking with our eyes or not, whether thoughts are occurring in the mind or not, the mere clarity of mind is never interrupted. This is what we call the all-ground consciousness, the origin of all our cognitions. For example, whether there are waves in the ocean or not, the water never changes. The ocean is always there. Sometimes there are strong waves, sometimes it is calm and placid, but there is not much difference; the water is still water. The wave-like six consciousnesses do sometimes arise, but the nature of the mind is still the nature of the mind. Whether we are sleeping, working during the day, having a conversation, or doing nothing at all, the ground consciousness is always present.

As one aspect of the eighth consciousness there is afflicted mind, the seventh consciousness. In the ground consciousness, there is subtle attachment—a stable, continuously present conception of self that makes a distinction between self and other. This is the afflicted mind. Although it is not actually a strong affliction in itself, it is the root of the afflictions, which is why it is called the afflicted mind. This is present in all sentient beings until they reach the seventh bodhisattva level. Beings abandon this consciousness once they attain the seventh bodhisattva level.

When we distinguish appearances and the perceived object, the objects of the five gate consciousnesses are perceived objects. The object of the sixth consciousness is appearances. The five sensory consciousnesses experience attractive and unattractive objects, but the sixth, mental consciousness experiences greed for attractive objects, aversion to unattractive objects, and delusion regarding neutral objects.

Since the five sense consciousnesses are nonconceptual, they do not experience much greed for attractive objects, nor do they experience much aversion toward unattractive objects. They are like cameras. If you take a picture of something nice with a camera, the picture stays in the camera, but the camera does not really think of it as being nice. If you take a picture of something ugly, the camera does not think of it as ugly. Similarly, the five sense consciousnesses of the eye, ear, nose, tongue, and body do not have any thought of good or bad. They just perceive.

The one who experiences greed for attractive objects, aversion toward unattractive objects, and delusion regarding neutral objects is the sixth, mental consciousness. When the eye sees a beautiful form, the sixth, mental consciousness thinks of it as good and produces greed. When it sees something unattractive, it thinks of it as bad and produces aversion. When we say it experiences delusion in relation to a neutral object, there is no coarse thought that is delusion, but it does not really know that this is an appearance in the mind or that that appearances are empty. Its essence is delusion. The thoughts of greed, aversion, and delusion that are like loquacious blind people toward the meaning generalities that appear in the sixth, mental consciousness are just mind. They do not actually see the external object.

Which consciousnesses do we use when we meditate? We do not meditate with the five sense consciousnesses. The five sense consciousness just perceive whatever appears to them, but there's nothing really there to meditate on. It's all emptiness, but there's no need to meditate on them. What needs to meditate is the sixth, mental consciousness. Because that is what can think of anything at all, we meditate with the sixth, mental consciousness.

The story of Nyama Paldarbum from *The Hundred Thousand Songs of Milarepa* explains how to meditate very clearly. When Paldarbum met Milarepa, she asked many questions—Where do you come from? Where are you going? How do you meditate? Who is your lama? Milarepa replied to each of her questions with a song. Paldarbum felt great faith and invited Milarepa to her home. When they got there, Paldarbum asked, "In the night time, I have to sleep, and in the day time I have to work. From morning till night I chase after food and clothing. I need to practice the Dharma and reach buddhahood. Just giving up isn't any good. Please teach me the Dharma that will bring me to buddhahood."

Milarepa responded with a song that taught five points through four analogies. One of the analogies is of the ocean:

> Take the great ocean as an example,
> And meditate without ups or downs.
> Take your own mind as the object,
> And meditate without suspicions.

Milarepa is saying that you should look at the ocean and see what it is like when there are no ups and downs of waves. Your meditation should be like the ocean with no waves. As in that analogy, you should look at your own mind and not have many thoughts or suspicions. As I mentioned above, the sixth, mental consciousness feels greed for attractive things, aversion to unattractive things, and delusion about neutral things. Free of those, you should meditate calmly and placidly within the ground consciousness.

Nyama Paldarbum replied:

> It's easy to meditate on the ocean,
> But not so easy to meditate on waves.
> Now tell me how to meditate on waves.
> It's easy to meditate on my own mind,
> But not so easy to meditate on thoughts.
> Now tell me how to meditate on thoughts.

Milarepa answered:

> If it's easy to meditate on the ocean,
> Waves are the magic of the ocean.
> Rest in the nature of the ocean itself.
> If it's easy to meditate on your own mind,
> Thoughts are the magic of the mind.
> Rest in the nature of mind-essence itself.

Thoughts are just displays of the mind. They may be waves stirring up the all-ground consciousness, but this is not a fault. If you just rest loosely in them, they will disappear right there. This is why when we meditate we should let the thoughts that occur in the sixth, mental consciousness relax into the all-ground consciousness.

EXPERIENCING APPEARANCES AS MIND

Here we have identified perceived objects and appearances. Perceived objects are external things such as form and sound, and appearances are the thoughts, afflictions, and feelings that appear internally in our mind. These two are different, and we need to distinguish between them.

> Perceived objects, such as form, sound, and so forth, have appeared due to mind, but they are not mind—they are the shared appearances of sentient beings and do not possess any true existence, besides being phenomena of dependent origination.

The perceived objects of external form, sound, and so forth naturally appear due to the power of our mind, but they are not themselves actually mind. Instead, these appearances are shared by many sentient beings and occur through interdependence. They appear while at the same time being empty. There is nothing about them that can be truly established; there is no solid thing that can be proven to truly exist. They just naturally appear through interdependence as the common experience of sentient beings.

For example, think of the river Ganges. It is not mind; it is water. You might go there some morning at dawn, rent a boat, and glide lazily up and down the river. It is nice, peaceful, and lovely, and you feel happy. That happiness is mind. Or you might see raw sewage and corpses floating in the river, and feel disgusted and depressed. That depression is mind. This is the distinction. The river Ganges is the perceived object. The feelings of happiness and depression are appearances. So perceived objects are not mind, but appearances are.

It is easy to understand that appearances—thoughts, feelings, and so forth—are mind. When we feel pleasure, that is obviously mind, and when we feel something that is not pleasure, such as aversion, that is clearly mind. It is easy to see that thoughts and feelings of pleasure or pain are mind. This is very easy to know and prove logically. It is very easy to meditate upon this.

However, when we consider external objects, it is more difficult. We could prove that external objects are mind through the reasoning of the mind-only school. We can use examples of dreams and so forth to come to understand that things are mind. In this respect it is easy to understand intellectually through study. But to really have an experience of it is much more difficult. We might think everything out there is mind, but taking it as the path of direct perception and directly meditating on it is very difficult. That is why this teaching differentiates between appearances—thoughts and feelings—and perceived objects. What this teaches is that the perceived object is not mind, but perceptions are.

The Ninth Karmapa's teachings in *Pointing Out the Dharmakaya* have five sections on the view. These are viewing the mind in stillness, viewing the mind in motion, viewing the mind in relation to appearances, viewing whether the moving and still minds are the same or different, and viewing whether mind and body are the same or different. There are these five different sections. Of these five different sections, people generally say that viewing the mind in stillness is the easiest. It is easy to contemplate, it is easy to meditate upon, and it is easy to gain an experience of it. Viewing the mind in motion is also pretty easy, but viewing the mind in relation to appearances is difficult in all respects: it is difficult to understand, it is difficult to meditate upon, and it is difficult to gain any experience of it.

Why is it so hard to experience external things as mind? It is because when an external object appears, it appears pretty much the same way whether there are five people looking at it, or six, or seven, or eight people looking at it. Everyone who looks at one object will say it is more or less the same sort of thing. We all think we are looking at the one, same thing, and this one thing does not seem like mind at all. We have a habitual tendency not to see it as mind, so it is not easy to meditate on it as mind. Many people tell me that meditating on external things as mind is very difficult. Some people might say that it is not so hard, but often they are speaking out of intellectual understanding, not experience.

Because of our habitual tendencies, when several people look at a single thing such as a table, they will all say that there is one table there. He sees it; she sees it; I see it. We all see the same table. But if we examine it, the actual appearance is different in each of our minds. It is not really out there. For example, if you have five televisions tuned to same channel, when you look at them, they all look exactly the same. They are all showing the same scenery, the same interior of the house, the same person is walking across it, and we would say that the televisions are all showing the same thing. But are they really the same thing? They are not—one is over here, and one is over there. They are not the same. Similarly, many people might see a single thing, but the image of that thing that appears to me does not appear to someone else. What appears to someone else does not appear to me. That is why we sometimes have to ask others, "Hey, did you see that?" If we all saw the same appearances we would not have to ask—if I saw it, you must have seen it, too. But that is not how it is. This is why everything we see is mind.

However, in order to make it easy to understand, these instructions do not explain it in this way. These instructions say that perceived objects are not mind, but that the feelings, thoughts, and things that arise in our mind are. When these instructions say that appearances are mind, they mean the latter—the feelings and thoughts.

While the presentations in mahamudra teachings and Khenpo Gangshar's instructions might seem contradictory, the two approaches are actually very similar. What is most important in the mahamudra instructions is that they are mind instructions: they tell us how to look at our mind, see what it is like, and see where it is. The instructions on dzogchen also give mind instructions, telling us how to look at the mind and see what it is like. In both the mahamudra and dzogchen traditions, what is most important is meditating on the mind, and both explain the reasons why we should meditate on the mind and the benefits of doing so.

7

LOOKING AT THE MIND

THE MIND IS THE ROOT of everything, but what is it like? Does the mind exist or not? Is it something, or nothing? Often we examine things like this with logical inference as in middle-way philosophy, but these instructions teach a different way to examine and analyze the mind. In the middle way, we examine it through logic and inference: we think that something must be so or not so. It is as if we were circling the mind from afar. Here, in the mind instructions, we do not examine the mind from afar with logical analysis. We instead look directly at it and take direct perception as the path. If there is a mind that exists, where is it? Is it in our head? Is it in our body? Is it something that is outside our body? We need to actually search for it, just looking, without using logic. We should not ask, what is it like and what proves it? In this way, the analytic meditation of a pandita differs from middle-way logic.

In the middle way, there are different types of reasoning, including logic that analyzes causes, logic that analyzes results, and analyses of the essence of phenomena, but the primary logic of the middle way is the logic of analyzing interdependence. This was the main line of reasoning taught by the noble Nagarjuna in his *Fundamental Wisdom of the Middle Way.* In the context of this logic, interdependence does not refer to the twelve links of interdependence. Instead, what it means is that any one thing arises in dependence upon something else. This is something we can examine logically. As Nagarjuna says:

Because there is no dharma at all
That is not interdependent,
Therefore there is no dharma at all
That is not emptiness.

There is nothing other than interdependence, and since there is only interdependence, there are no things that are not empty.

I often demonstrate this with the example of incense sticks. If you have two sticks of incense, one of which is two inches and the other six, you would have to say that the six-inch stick is long and the two-inch stick is short. Everyone will agree that the two-inch stick is short, not long, and that the six-inch stick is long, not short. But if you compare the six-inch stick to a twelve-inch stick, then suddenly it has become short. Whether something is short or long depends on what you compare it with. In this way, there is no long or short—long and short are empty. Similarly, there is no big or small, no good or bad, and no here or there. All of these are just labels given in relation to one another; they cannot be truly established and therefore they are empty.

When we think like this, we can know that there is no such thing as long and understand that long is empty. But this does not come from experience; it comes from understanding. We have an understanding that things are probably empty and they probably do not truly exist. If we meditate on this understanding for a long time, we can develop certainty in it, and then we continue to meditate on that. This is a long and slow process; it takes a long time to arrive at actual realization—we cannot realize the dharma nature quickly. This is why the Buddha taught in the sutras that it takes three uncountable aeons of gathering merit before we can reach enlightenment. It is a long and slow process of first developing an understanding of emptiness, meditating, and developing certainty. Then we meditate as we gather merit, but we cannot develop this quickly.

In the secret mantra vajrayana, however, it is said that we can attain the state of unified Vajradhara in one lifetime and one body. How can that be possible if the sutras say it takes three uncountable aeons?

If you follow the path of the sutras, it does take three uncountable aeons, but if you take a different path—the path of the secret mantra vajrayana—it is possible to achieve the ultimate result in one lifetime and one body. The difference is that we do not just take logic and inference as the path; we do it through experience. We look to see where our mind is and what it is like. When we do this we see that the mind is naturally empty of any essence. The mind seems to be something, but when we look for it, we cannot find it either inside or outside our bodies. We should not merely analyze it; we must look at it directly and experience it. When we experience it, we do not need to prove that it is emptiness through reasoning, we simply have the feeling that it is emptiness.

The meditation practices of the middle way and the analytic meditation of the pandita both come to the same fundamental point, but they do so by different methods. In the middle way, one does this by engaging one's understanding and examining external phenomena conceptually. This can bring us to the understanding that everything is emptiness, but meditating on that does not really lead to actual experience. In the meditations of the pandita and the kusulu, however, we do not look at external things conceptually but instead look inward at our own internal experience.

We can think of this through an analogy—the distinction is like the difference between the methods of historians and archaeologists. A historian will read all the history books and might perhaps know that the Buddha came to Sarnath in northern India and turned the wheel of Dharma. They will have the feeling they know this, but they do not have any actual experience of it. The archaeologist will actually go to Sarnath, dig in the ground, and find all sorts of signs and indications. They will look at a stone here, an ornament there, and an inscription here. When they dig through it all, they find the Ashoka pillar and see all the writing on it, which they then read and see that it says that this is the place where the Buddha first turned the wheel of Dharma. After they do this, they think to themselves, "Wow! This really is the place where the Lord Buddha taught the Dharma!" In addition to an understanding and conceptual certainty, they also have a concrete experience.

Similarly, when we meditate we don't merely think that every-thing is emptiness. Rather, we look and see what the mind is like. Where is it? Where does it dwell? Where does it go? What is its essence? When we look carefully, we can have an experience where we feel that the nature of mind really is like that. It really is empty. That is why we do the analytic meditation of the pandita.

LOOKING FOR THE MIND IN THE BODY

Khenpo Gangshar begins the actual instructions on how to do the analytic meditation of a pandita by saying:

> You should now examine where this mind dwells: from the top of the hair on your head to the nails on your toes; from the outer layer of skin, the flesh in between, to the bones, five organs, and six vessels within.

We have a mind that seems strong and powerful. We think that there is a mind, and that it is the root of all appearances—but where is it? How does it exist? We think that our sixth, mental consciousness, our mind that can think of anything at all and has the essence of greed, aversion, and delusion is something that exists somewhere. We need to look carefully to see where it is.

We first look for the mind in our body. We start from our head—the tips of our hair, the middle of the hair, the roots, the skin of the scalp. Is our mind there? Is it in our skull? Is it in the brain within the skull? Is it someplace in our neck or spinal column? We look throughout our entire body from our head through our torso to our legs, feet, toes, toenails, and out to the very tips of our toenails to see if we can find our mind. If our mind were something that existed, there would have to be someplace we could point to and say, "This is where my mind is!" It would have a shape and a color, and we could say, "It is such and such a color and has such and such a shape." But when we look, we cannot see it anywhere. We can look out our skin on the outside, the flesh in the middle, and the marrow of our bones to see where the mind is, but we cannot find it. We do not examine this with logic. Instead, we actually look. If we use logic, we will come to an understanding of it, but that is not what we are doing here. Here we are looking at it directly. We should be like zoologists studying birds in the wild. When scientists study birds, they go outside and watch: Where did the bird fly to? When did the bird go? What does the bird eat? When does the bird leave its nest in the morning? When does it come back to its nest in the evening? These scientists actually look and see for themselves what the bird does. We need to be like them: we need to look at our mind and we need to see—Where is the mind? Is the mind in our feet? Is it in our head? Where is it? What is it like? Is it inside or outside? We need to look and see for ourselves.

> When investigating the dwelling place of mind, most Chinese will claim that it abides in the head. Tibetans will say that it dwells in the heart. Neither one is sure because when you touch the top of the head the mind seems to leap there and when you touch the soles of the feet it seems to jump there.

When Khenpo Gangshar gave these instructions, he often taught them to Tibetans, but he also sometimes taught them to Chinese. When he asked them where the mind was, they would give different answers. The Chinese at that time had received some scientific education and would answer that the mind is in the brain or the head. Tibetans, however, would say it is in the heart because that is the center of the body. Although they would feel this and say this, neither is true. It is not really in either place because if you look for exactly where it is, you cannot find it. It is not really in the head or the brain. Perhaps since thoughts occur through the support of the channels within the brain, the brain may be a basis for the mind, but the brain is not the mind itself. It is material. When a person dies, the brain is still there, but the mind is not. Thus the mind is not in the brain. Similarly, it is not really in the heart, because it seems as if it were present in the whole body and not concentrated in the center.

We have both mind and thoughts. In the abhidharma, mind, or cognition, is considered the aggregate of consciousness, but thoughts are categorized under the aggregate of formations. Within the aggregate of formations, there are fifty-one different formations. In our Buddhist instructions, we generally say that such thoughts are in the brain. The reason comes from the meditation on the peaceful and wrathful deities. In their pure form, there are the forty-two peaceful deities, but in their impure form they are the eight consciousnesses, which are present at the center of the body, in the heart. This is why we meditate on the peaceful deities such as Vairochana and the rest of the five dhyani buddhas as well as the five female buddhas and so forth in the heart. In terms of thoughts, there are the fifty-one formations: feeling, conception, virtuous thoughts (virtuous mental factors), unvirtuous thoughts (unvirtuous mental factors), strong afflictions, minor afflictions, and also changeable mental factors. These occur in the brain because the brain provides the conditions for them to occur. In the practice of the peaceful and wrathful deities, we meditate on the fifty-one bloodthirsty, wrathful deities in the brain. Thus the cause for the fifty-one mental factors is most likely in the brain, but cognition, which is essentially clear awareness that can go anywhere, is not necessarily located there.

So the mind is not necessarily in either the brain or the heart. As Khenpo Gangshar says, when you feel something or think about something, the mind jumps there. If you have a sensation in your head, your mind leaps there. When you touch the soles of your feet, the mind jumps there. If you wiggle your finger, then at that point the mind seems to be in the finger, but if you do something else, the mind goes elsewhere. The mind seems to be throughout the body, but exactly *where* is uncertain—it does not dwell in any fixed location. The mind seems to go wherever you experience a sensation, so you cannot say with certainty that it is in either the head or the heart. This is looking inside the body.

INVESTIGATING WHERE THE MIND DWELLS

We cannot find any place inside the body where the mind dwells, so we might think that the mind dwells in external objects—the forms we see, sounds we hear, scents we smell, and so forth. So we need to look and see whether the mind actually resides in them. Does the mind somehow exit the body and reside in the object? When we examine this, although we see and hear things, we cannot find that the mind dwells in external objects. As Khenpo Gangshar says:

> It has no fixed place. It dwells neither inside outer objects nor inside the body, nor in the empty space in between. You must become certain that it has no dwelling place.

Sometimes it seems as if the mind is outside someplace. We see all these things outside. We see mountains or we hear echoes off of cliffs. We have all these different thoughts of different places, and the mind seems to go to those places when we think about them. But it only seems that way; the mind is not really outside of us either. It dwells neither in external objects nor someplace in the body—we cannot find any place in the body where it is. You might then think that since it is not in the body and it is not outside the body, it must be in the empty space in between. But if you look, you cannot find it. We need to look and become certain that the mind has no dwelling place—we must be certain that there is no real place that we can we can point to and say, "Aha! That's where it is!"

Khenpo Gangshar continues:

> If your mind has a dwelling place, what are the outer, inner, and middle aspects of this dwelling place? Is it identical with or different from the dweller?
>
> If they are identical—since there is increase or decrease, change and alteration in outer objects and within the body—your mind will change in the very same way. So it is illogical to think they are identical.
>
> If they are different, then is the essence of this different mind something that exists or not? If it is, then it should at least have a shape and color. Since there is no shape or color, it does not unilaterally exist. However, since this "Ever-conscious and Ever-aware King" is unceasing, it does not unilaterally not exist.

If your mind were to have a dwelling place, what would it be like? Is it the same as the mind, or different? If it were the same, since external objects change, the mind would have to change in the same way. External things get bigger or smaller. They change in various ways. If they were the same as the mind, then the mind would get bigger or smaller, or change in the same ways. Also, sometimes that outside object is there, but sometimes it is not. If the mind were the same as the object, it would follow that when the object is there the mind would also be present, but when the object is not there, the mind would be absent. So it is illogical to think that they are identical. But if the mind and the object are different, is the essence of this different mind something that exists, or not? If so, we should be able to say, "This is what the mind is. This is where it dwells." The mind that dwells somewhere should have a color and shape of some sort. But it has none, so we cannot say that it really exists.

Neither Something nor Nothing: The Emptiness of the Mind

If our mind were something that existed, there would have to be some place that it stayed and there would have to be something that stayed there. We would be able to say, "That is where it is! The essence of my mind is this! My mind is staying here." There would be something we could find and point to, but there's nothing like that. We cannot say that we see our mind in some particular place. We can't say anything like that. If it were some existing thing, it would have color and shape, or there would have to be some identifiable thing that does not have shape or color. We cannot find any thing with a shape or any thing with a color, and if we look for a thing that has neither shape nor color, we cannot find such a thing anywhere.

Our mind is our own, so if there were something to find we should be able to find it, but we cannot. When we look for our hand, for example, we can point to our hand and say, "This is my hand. See, these are my five fingers." But our mind is not like that. If we look to see if it is outside the body, inside, in our feet, in our head, or anywhere else, we cannot find anything at all. It is as if the mind were not there, as if it did not exist. When we look for our mind and cannot find it, it is not because we do not know how to look. It is not because we are incapable of looking for our mind. We have a mind that can think anything at all, so where is it? It is the root of all our actions, good and ill. But we cannot find the mind, because its essence is naturally empty.

This is why the sutras teach outer emptiness, inner emptiness, outer and inner emptiness, and so forth. The mind is not far away. The emptiness of our mind means that we cannot find the mind anywhere at all, and this is also what the sutras teach. It is similar with the middle way: we could use logic and reasoning to prove that the mind is emptiness, but when we look at it, we realize that the lack of anything to find is what the middle way means by emptiness. For this reason, the mind is empty. This is what we discover when we look at it from the perspective of emptiness.

When we say that appearances are mind and the mind is empty, this means that it is as if the mind did not exist. We are not merely proving it through scriptural citations or logic. We actually have to experience it: we have to look at it. We have to see: What is it like? When we look, what do we see? We cannot see or find anything. That is what it means to say the mind is empty.

But the emptiness is spontaneously present. We cannot really say the mind is nothing. It is not as if the mind cannot see or feel anything; it is not as if it cannot do anything. It is not just a blank nothingness. There is the potential for all sorts of appearances to arise. There is the capacity for qualities and wisdom to arise. This is what we call the spontaneous presence of emptiness. It is what Khenpo Gangshar calls the "ever-conscious and ever-aware king." The mind is able to know anything, see anything, feel anything, and experience anything. It can know and be aware of anything—it is as strong and powerful as a king.

This mind that understands, remembers the past, and thinks, is unceasing. It never stops. It is present, even though we cannot find it. Does this mean it is something? It does not, because it is empty—we cannot find it. But that does not mean that it is nothing, a blank void. It can understand anything. It can think, engage in conversation, and do anything. It is unceasing. If we did not have a mind, our body would be little more than a corpse. But it is not like that. We can do things with this body. It is as if the mind did exist. Its essence is not something, but it is not nothing either. We look and look, search and search, and can't find anything, but there is something that knows and is aware. There is something that can see, hear, and know anything, and that is unceasing, so you cannot say that it does not exist at all.

This is why many scholars cite this verse:

While this appearance is not established appearance,
It has no basis and no root.
While this emptiness is not established emptiness
Interdependence occurs unceasingly.

When we look at something such as a glass, it is empty—there is nothing there that truly exists. But even though it is empty, it appears to us. Similarly, the mind thinks, knows, remembers, and does many things, but at the same time as it thinks, knows, and remembers, it is not there. What is the nature of the mind like? It is not anything. But while it is not anything, there is something that sees and knows. However, if you look for it while it sees and knows something, there's nothing to find. This is the characteristic of the mind. When we experience this as it is, this is not just a conceptual understanding of what it must be like. When we actually experience what the mind is truly like, this is what it means to say that appearances are mind, mind is empty, and emptiness is spontaneously present.

We also say that this spontaneous presence is self-liberated. Normally we are confused by the appearances we perceive, but when we realize the spontaneous presence of emptiness, we are no longer confused by appearances. We naturally realize that they dwell within the nature of emptiness and there is no longer anything about them that can bind us to either samsara or conceptual thoughts.

Should we think the mind is empty and meditate on that? That is not what we should do. You might think that the mind that can think and remembers anything is unceasing, so we need to meditate on that. But that is not necessary, either. Instead, we simply need to look at the mind and see it as it is: essentially empty, but unceasingly thinking and aware. This is the characteristic of the mind. We do not need to meditate thinking that nothingness is something, or that something is nothing. Instead, we just need to know its essence. This should not just be a mental understanding; it is important that we know the nature of the mind as it is.

The Third Karmapa, Rangjung Dorje, described this in his "Aspiration Prayer of Mahamudra":

> Not something, even the victors cannot see it.
> Not nothing, it is the ground of all samsara and nirvana.
> This is not a contradiction; it is unity, the middle way.
> May we realize the mind's nature, beyond extremes.

When we look to see where the essence of our mind is, there is nothing we can see or locate. There is no color, no shape, and nothing to find. It is not something. There's nothing there. It is not that the mind is too small and we cannot see it. It is not that it is too pure for us to see. It is not that it is too far away for us to see. It is not because we are just ignorant and do not know how to look. It is not any of these: even the victors—the wise and omniscient buddhas—cannot see or find anything about the nature of the mind that can be established as a thing. The mind is not something that exists in any way. Just as there is nothing we can see, there is nothing the buddhas can see either. This is because the nature of mind is emptiness.

For example, when the Buddha taught emptiness, he taught about many different kinds of emptiness: outer emptiness, inner emptiness, outer and inner emptiness, and so forth. Even the victorious buddhas cannot see these. The reason they cannot see them is not because the buddhas lack knowledge or intelligence; it is because the essence of those emptinesses itself is empty.

Normally we think that if a thing is empty, it must be nothingness—a blank void, nothing at all. We think of it as being like the inanimate void of empty space. But if we look at the mind and ask ourselves if it is nothing, it is not. As Rangjung Dorje says in the second line of the stanza cited above, "Not nothing, it is the ground of all samsara and nirvana." It is the root of everything. When we wander in samsara, see the appearances of the six classes of samsara, experience suffering and afflictions, and have problems and difficul-

LOOKING AT THE MIND

ties, all of it happens on the basis of our mind. When we free ourselves of the suffering of samsara and achieve nirvana, the ground for
the wisdom of the buddhas and their activity for the sake of sentient
beings is also just this mind. For that reason, the mind is not unilaterally nothing. If it were, we would become like corpses or rocks, but
we do not. Wandering in samsara is just a projection of the mind.
Achieving buddhahood as well is just what happens when the nature
of the mind becomes manifest as it is. The basis of both samsara and
nirvana is the mind, so the mind is not nothing.

So when Rangjung Dorje says "Not something, it is not seen even
by the buddhas," it means the same thing as when Khenpo Gangshar
says that if mind exists, "then it should at least have a shape and color.
Since there is no shape or color, it does not unilaterally exist." When
Rangjung Dorje says, "Not nothing, it is the ground of all samsara and
nirvana," it means the same as when Khenpo Gangshar says, "However, since this 'Ever-conscious and Ever-aware King' is unceasing, it
does not unilaterally not exist." These both teach what the essence of
our mind is like.

This might sound like a contradiction. If we are scholars studying
logically, we think that a phenomenon has to be either something or
nothing; it cannot be both. If it is not something, it must be nothing. If it is not nothing, it must be something. These are mutually
exclusive and there can be no third alternative. There is no other way
that it can be. But actually, when we look at the nature of the mind,
not being something and not being nothing are not contradictory.
Our mind is clear and can know things. But at the same time if we
look to see where it is, we cannot find it anywhere. Therefore it is
not something, but it is still knowing, so it cannot be nothing either. These two points are not contradictory; they go together. Even
though it does not exist, the mind knows, sees, and understands—it
is the all-knowing, all-aware king. Still, we cannot find it. These two
are brought together and unified; this is the great middle way.

When we engage in logical analysis, we often present the dharma
expanse or emptiness as having the characteristic of being neither
something nor nothing. If we ask what has this characteristic, without needing to analyze and examine, we see that it is present within

our minds. The mind is not something and it is not nothing. It dwells neither in the extreme of existence nor in the extreme of nonexistence. The middle way of unity is present within our mind. Is this something we need to experience from far away? It is not—the nature of mind is not far away from us. Nor is it something that we have to go through great trials and tribulations to find. It is our mind as it is. We do not need to make something into nothing or to make nothing into something. The nature of the mind is not something that occurs because we meditate. It is not something that only happens when we examine it. It is not something that the Buddha or anyone else made that way. It is just the way the mind is—its nature.

8

A SUMMARY OF THE
ANALYTIC MEDITATION
OF A PANDITA

W E ALL STRIVE TO FIND happiness and avoid suffering. In
order to find happiness and avoid suffering, we need to be careful about karma, cause, and effect. Karma, cause, and effect function
through our bodies, speech, and minds, but the most important of
these is our mind. So we need to know the nature of this mind thoroughly. We need to look to see where it is. We need to recognize the
nature of the mind as it is, without altering it. Just resting in meditation within that is enough. This is how we come to understand the
way the mind is.

> The explanation up to this point completes the preliminary
> teachings of the analytical meditation of a pandita.

Of the two main parts of the instructions, the first, the analytic meditation of a pandita, has been completed. When we examine where the
mind comes from, where it dwells, and where it goes to, we see that
the mind cannot be established as a truly existing thing. But it is also
not nothing at all. Many Buddhist philosophical texts give examples
of things that do not exist in any way, shape, or form, such as rabbit
horns or flowers that grow in the sky, but the mind-essence is not
like that. Its essence of being clear wisdom is unceasing and this is

something that we can actually experience. We do the analytic meditation of the pandita in order to recognize this.

If you look on the surface, it seems as if this is probably analyzing through logic and inference. But it is not that. Actually, it is looking to see where the mind is and experiencing it through direct perception. But how do we look at it?

The texts on valid perception teach four different types of direct perception. The first is direct sensory perception, such as when we actually see with our eyes, actually hear with our ears, actually smell a scent with our noses, actually taste a flavor with our tongues, or actually feel a touch with our bodies. The actual experience of an external object through the five sense faculties is what we call direct sensory perception. Is the analytic meditation of the pandita direct sensory perception? It is not.

The second is direct mental perception. There is a slight occurrence of a nonconceptual mental consciousness that forms a link between the sensory consciousnesses and the conceptual mental consciousness. Is this it? This is also not it. Both direct sensory and direct mental perception are directed outward at external objects. They do not look inward at the internal mind.

Is the analytic meditation of the pandita self-aware direct perception? It is not. Self-awareness as described in the texts on validity means that the mind is not hidden from itself. It does not look out at the external object; it looks at the inner mind. But between the unconfused nature and the confused perceptions, it looks at confused perceptions. It is knowing what we see. When we hear something, it is knowing that we hear. When we think about something, knowing that we think about it is what we call the self-aware direct perception. This is not the analytic meditation of the pandita either.

Well then, when we do the analytic meditation of a pandita and examine our mind to see where it comes from, where it dwells, and where it goes, what sort of direct perception do we use? We use direct yogic perception. Through our samadhi and the intelligence born of meditation, we actually experience the way the mind is: neither something nor nothing. We do not contrive it through inference, through thinking "It is empty." Instead, we experience it directly. It is our own mind, and when we look at the essence of our own mind, if it were something, there would be a thing we could find. But we don't find anything. Well then, is it nothing at all, like space? It is not. Clear awareness is unceasing, and actually directly experiencing this essence is the result of the analytic meditation of the pandita.

This talk of the four types of direct perception generally comes up in intellectual discussion on the topic of validity. However, when we combine that with our meditation, we see that our insight is not direct sensory perception, not self-aware direct perception, and not inference. It is direct yogic perception. The nature of the mind is something we have to directly experience in meditation; we should not let it be stained by inference. If we were to think about it through inference, that would not be the right samadhi on the nature of the mind. So the discussion of direct yogic perception may be rather intellectual, but it is also very helpful for our meditation.

PART THREE
THE RESTING MEDITATION OF A KUSULU

THE SECOND PART OF KHENPO GANGSHAR'S INSTRUCTIONS is the main practice, the resting meditation of a kusulu. A kusulu is someone who leads a very simple, uncomplicated life and does things easily and without much effort. Similarly, in the resting meditation of a kusulu, we do not go through a lot of effort to do the meditation. It is not examining anything thoroughly, it is not studying; we just rest simply in equipoise just as it is. This is extremely important.

The reason is that the realization of the nature of the mind is not something that we can find by searching for it from afar. It is present within the essence of the mind itself. If we do not alter or change that in any way, that is enough. It is not as if we were lacking something before so we need to make something new through our meditation. It is not as if we are bad and have to go through all sorts of efforts to make ourselves good. Goodness is something we all have. It has always been present within all of us, but we have just not looked for it or seen it yet, so we have become confused. Therefore all we need to do is to just rest within it without changing it. We see where it stays and rest there, so we are like a kusulu. This means that we rest free and easy with nothing to do, very simply. We do not need to think that we are making something good or that we need to meditate properly. It is enough just to know what we already have.

Well then, what do we need to do? We just need to recognize the way our mind is as it is and then rest in equipoise within that, as it is. In the instructions on mahamudra, this is what we call ordinary mind. This is just knowing how our mind is and what its essence is like, and then resting in equipoise within that. Sometimes we call this the natural state, which just means that we do not change it in any way. Both of these terms mean that we do not analyze or examine too much, nor do we alter things at all. We simply rest in the nature of the mind as it is. That is what we call resting meditation. Resting here means we leave it alone. We don't need to do a lot to it or alter it in any way. Just rest in equipoise within its essence, whatever that is like.

9

DEVOTION AND
STABILITY

WHAT IS THE MOST important thing when we practice meditation? Devotion is most important, as the "Short Vajradhara
Lineage Prayer" teaches:

> Devotion's the head of meditation, as it's taught.
> As ones who pray always to the lama who opens
> The gate to the treasury of oral instructions,
> Please bless us that genuine devotion arise.

It is crucial for our meditation to have devotion. If our devotion is
strong, our meditation will also be strong. If our devotion is not so
strong, our meditation will not be strong either. If we have one hundred percent devotion, our meditation will also be one hundred percent. Similarly, if we have fifty percent devotion, we will have only
fifty percent meditation, and if we only have one percent devotion,
then we will only have one percent meditation. This is why devotion
is so important for our practice.

You might think that the importance of devotion is taught for
people of lesser capabilities who are not very smart. You might think
it is blind faith. But that is not the case. If we have strong devotion and conviction in the Dharma, we will be diligent about our
Dharma practice and be able to do it. Without faith or devotion, we
will not really be able to practice or to be diligent. Since diligence is

so important, it is critical that we have strong devotion and strong conviction in the Dharma.

You might think you ought to have faith in your lama. When you see the lama's good qualities, you have faith in them, but sometimes you also see faults in the lama, and then how can you have faith? Should you pretend that a lama who does not have good qualities actually does and then develop faith? Should you pretend that your lama has no faults even though you see faults? You should not do either of these. It is possible that your lama can have both good qualities and faults. You should not have faith in your lama just because they exhibit good behavior, are upstanding, and are a good person. You should not have faith in a lama thinking that their faults aren't really faults. If your lama has faults, that does not make any difference. If the lama has good qualities, that is good. But those are not the reasons why we should be devoted to our lamas.

The reason to have devotion to the lama is the Dharma that they teach—that is the thing that can bring us to the ultimate results of liberation and omniscience. That is what we really need; because of that Dharma we will naturally be able to benefit ourselves and others spontaneously. This is what is most important, and this is why we must have devotion.

If you read the life story of the great yogi Milarepa, you will see what extraordinary faith and devotion he had in his guru, Marpa the Translator. Because of his devotion, he was able to take his meditation and practice to their ultimate end, through which he attained the supreme and ordinary accomplishments. But how did he develop such extraordinary faith and devotion? First he realized that Marpa was a teacher who had the extraordinary instructions on mahamudra and the six yogas that the great Naropa had taught. He had extraordinary confidence in these, through which he developed his devotion. He saw that Marpa could teach him the Dharma that he needed to help himself. There were times when Marpa treated him terribly and beat him harshly, and it is not as if Milarepa did not feel any pain. It is not as if he were always happy. He was often discouraged—he thought he would never receive the Dharma instructions he needed. He got extremely depressed and cried on many occasions. He even gave up and left a few times, thinking he would never receive any Dharma teachings. Is this because he lacked faith in Marpa? It is not. He did not develop his faith thinking that Marpa was a fine, upstanding, and admirable person. What he actually had faith in is that Marpa had truly profound Dharma instructions, and that these were the instructions that could benefit him. This is the level on which he had faith in Marpa. He had faith because he knew that if he could do the practice, he would be able to attain its results.

We should not look for a lama who has absolutely no faults and is replete with good qualities—we will never find anyone like that. We do need to have strong devotion, but the devotion is for the Dharma, not the lama's human character.

This devotion is very important to our meditation—it is the head of meditation, it is said. This is actually an excellent metaphor. When we think about our Dharma practice, there are two parts: our samadhi meditation and devotion. Devotion might seem like something small: we spend so much time in meditation that devotion seems insignificant in comparison. Similarly, the head is tiny in comparison to the rest of the human body, so we might think that the head cannot be very important. But without this little head, the big body would have no mouth and thus would be unable to eat. You would not have eyes, so you could not see. You would not have ears, so you could not listen to Dharma talks. Without a mouth you could not say a word. Thus without this one little thing, your body would be unable to do anything. But because you have a head, your body can actually do things. It is similar with meditation. Devotion might seem a small thing in comparison to the long time spent in meditation, but just as the body will not work without a head, your meditation will not go anywhere without devotion. If your devotion is strong, our practice will be strong. If your devotion is intense and you can practice with one hundred percent effort, that is wonderful. If you are not quite able to do that, then it is still excellent. But without that intensity of devotion you will not be able to practice in such a way as will bring you to the final result.

Devotion is important to our Dharma practice in general, but it is especially important for the analytic meditation of the pandita and the resting meditation of the kusulu. It is most important to know that we can do these practices. We need to think, "I can do this. I can do this meditation. I can develop real experience." Khenpo Gangshar's instructions have exceptional power and blessings that we can feel—they are not like other instructions. This is not because of any qualities on my part; it comes from the qualities and blessings of this exceptional lama and his instructions. But whether you can experience this depends on your own faith and confidence. If you have strong faith and devotion, you will be able to receive their blessings.

Sometimes people think too much: they might look at these instructions and think they are so easy that anyone can do them. How can anything so easy have such blessings? But if you practice with faith and devotion, these instructions will help you. Without faith and devotion, however, they will not do much for you. This is why faith, devotion, and belief are so important for our practice in general and crucial for these instructions on the analytic meditation of the pandita and the resting meditation of the kusulu in particular.

TRANQUILITY MEDITATION

In general, meditation instructions often teach both tranquility and insight meditation. Many presentations teach that one should practice tranquility meditation first and insight meditation later. But here we meditate on the two together. We are taught to meditate on the nature of things by looking directly at them. If we can do this, our mind will become peaceful and we will naturally develop tranquility meditation. At the same time, we will also develop the clarity of insight. In this way we do not separate tranquility and insight; we practice them together. But even though Khenpo Gangshar does not teach tranquility meditation explicitly, studying it can help us to develop the stability of our mind, so I think it is helpful to review tranquility meditation.

I have met many people who have received pointing-out instructions. Usually, when we receive pointing-out instructions, there is some sort of feeling or experience that happens. This is good and fine, but it may not be very stable. People who tell me what happened for them when they received the pointing-out instructions often say that they didn't recognize anything or that they recognized something and had some feeling, but it just dissipated. It changed and was not so helpful in the end. This is why it is important for us to identify both the stability of shamatha and the clarity of insight. Having the certainty that comes from study and reasoning will also help us develop strong meditation. This is why developing some stability through tranquility meditation is helpful.

The Difference between Tranquility and Insight Meditation

You might wonder what the difference between tranquility and insight meditation is. Tranquility meditation is just resting stably. There is not necessarily any intelligence present, whether the intelligence born of listening, contemplating, or wisdom. We do not really recognize the mind: we just rest peacefully free of thoughts within the empty aspect of the mind. That is tranquility or shamatha meditation. But when we know the nature of the mind clearly and thoroughly, then it is insight meditation. Insight has clarity. But it is good to have stability in our meditation, even if it lacks such clarity.

In *Clarifying the Natural State*, Takpo Tashi first teaches that we should sit up straight with good posture. Even before we are given any instructions on how to work with the mind, if we just sit for a few days practicing our posture, the mind will naturally come to rest. This will naturally bring out the stability of our minds.

Five Methods of Tranquility Meditation

Instructions on tranquility meditation often present two types of tranquility meditation: tranquility meditation with and without support. But if we leave that discussion aside, there are many other methods as well, among which are the nine methods for resting the mind. The first few are especially helpful for developing tranquility meditation, so I will discuss them here.

RESTING AND CONTINUAL RESTING

The first of the nine methods for resting the mind is simply called resting. Even when there are no thoughts occurring, the mind does not become blank, like a rock. There is still clarity that knows, but if you can rest for a short period without many thoughts, clear and sharp, that is resting. Since we do this meditation for only a short time, we have the thought of recognizing it—we think, "This is resting." This is the first method of resting the mind: just resting.

We should repeat this several times, just letting the mind rest. In the first method, we meditate for a short time over and over again, but we then need to develop our meditation. To do this, we just prolong it a bit. When we lengthen the duration of our meditation by just a little bit, this is what we call the second method, continual resting.

RETRIEVING AND RESTING

If your meditation immediately becomes great and sustained, that is wonderful, but sometimes that does not happen. Sometimes thoughts occur while we are meditating. When a thought does occur during your meditation, you should not get upset about it. You should not think that you are a terrible meditator or get discouraged in any way. You should not think that you are not doing it right—that is not at all necessary. On the other hand, if you follow thoughts that occur while you are meditating as they go on their merry little way, that does not work either. You cannot just keep on following the thoughts. Instead, you need to recognize what is happening. You need to recognize that you were resting, but then you had a thought and got distracted. Do not see that distraction as a fault or problem; just go back to how you were resting before. This is the third step, called retrieving and resting: put aside any thought that might have occurred and go back to your meditation.

Thus we have three different methods: resting, continually resting, and retrieving and resting. These are good methods to work with in your tranquility meditation; they will help you to develop stability in your meditation. But in meditating like this, we are not really looking at the essence of the mind. We are primarily working with stability when we practice tranquility.

TAMING AND PACIFYING

When we do shamatha regularly, sometimes a lot of thoughts will arise or we will not have much clarity of mind. When this happens, there are two different remedies: taming and pacifying.

When we have a lot of thoughts that we cannot stop, we need to think to ourselves, "From the time I was little until now, I have had millions of thoughts, but they have not helped me in any way." Sometimes our thoughts seem like they are important, but really they are not—there is no point to them. As the great master Shantideva said:

For those whose minds are slack and wandering
Are caught between the fangs of the afflictions.

People who have many thoughts also have many afflictions—they are caught in the maw of the afflictions just as if they were trapped between the fangs of a carnivorous beast. If this happens, you can look at all the thoughts and think that they are no good, that they are a problem. This is the method of taming: when we realize that we lack control over our mind, we should think about the faults of excessive thinking, and that will help to tame our minds.

The next method is pacifying. Pacifying means to think about the benefits of tranquility meditation. We realize that through the methods of tranquility meditation we can develop the real deep holding of samadhi; we will develop clarity and stability. This will be beneficial for us—we can gain control over our minds. When we reflect on the benefits of meditation again and again, we get excited and joyous about our meditation. This will help us to gain some discipline over our mind. This is the method of pacifying. When we find ourselves unable to control our minds, we should try practicing these methods of taming and pacification as a remedy.

These are five of the nine methods of resting the mind. They will be helpful for you in your meditation, as they will help you develop stability. This is not a situation where you necessarily have any recognition of the way things are—there may not be much clarity. It is merely resting stably and easily. This is tranquility meditation. It is on the support of that stability that we can develop insight meditation. Insight is meditation that has intelligence. Tranquility meditation by itself lacks intelligence, which is why it does not work as a true remedy for the afflictions.

The analytic meditation of the pandita discussed above differs from tranquility in that it is a way of coming to know the nature of the mind and seeing the mind's essence. It is seeing that mind cannot be established as anything, seeing that it has clarity, and also seeing the union of clarity and emptiness. Tranquility lacks this wisdom, but it does provide the basis on which we can develop the intelligence of insight meditation.

10

GETTING RIGHT DOWN TO MEDITATION

THERE ARE TWO PARTS to the instructions on the resting meditation of the kusulu. The first part is the instructions on resolving. The Tibetan word translated here as *resolving* literally means to climb straight over a pass without making switchbacks back and forth—it means to go directly there. Here it means to go right into samadhi meditation. The second part of the instructions is distinguishing mind from awareness. Sometimes we are distracted, and sometimes we are not. When we are distracted, that is mind, and when we are undistracted, that is awareness. When we are not distracted, it is very easy to know the nature of the mind. But when we are distracted, we have many different thoughts that prevent us from knowing the mind-essence. This is the aspect of confusion. "Distinguishing" means telling these two states apart.

For the main practice of the resting meditation of a kusulu, let your mind and body become comfortable, soft, and relaxed. Do not think of anything, and rest naturally. The important point here is that we do not think of anything. Do not think about the past and do not think about the future. Do not think of anything at all. You should not do this by tightening or gripping, but instead by being loose, relaxed, and comfortable. Just let yourself rest naturally within this, without thinking. In the analytic meditation of the pandita, there is an examination of where the mind is, what it is like, what color it is, and so forth. But here there is no such examination: let your mind rest loosely and naturally. Just look at whatever feelings arise.

RESTING THE BODY AND MIND

Khenpo Gangshar's instructions on insight meditation begin with four points on posture:

> Keep your body straight, refrain from talking, open your mouth slightly, and let the breath flow naturally.

The first instruction is to keep your body straight so that the mind will be clear. The second instruction is to refrain from talking. If we talk while meditating, we will have a lot of thoughts. It will be difficult for our minds to rest and be clear, so we refrain from talking. The third instruction is to open your mouth slightly. Don't close your mouth, but don't let it gape open either. This means to let your body relax. As the great Machig Labdrön said, "Let the four limbs relax." This is important for your meditation. The fourth instruction is to let the breath flow normally. If your breath is moving quickly, let it move quickly. If it is moving slowly, let it move slowly. Do not try to make your long breaths into short breaths; do not try to make short breaths into long breaths. Do not hold your breath or do anything else to it. However it is, just let it be, which means not to change it in any way. These four points tell us how to let the body rest. There is no effort of the body that would produce many thoughts in the mind. This is taught so that we will be able to clearly recognize the nature of the mind.

In addition to these, Khenpo Gangshar also teaches methods for resting the mind:

> Don't pursue the past and don't invite the future. Simply rest naturally in the naked ordinary mind of the immediate present without trying to correct it or "re-place" it.

The instruction here is that external appearances, whatever they may be, do not really hurt us. It all comes down to the mind. Is the mind some hardened, solid lump to which we cannot do anything at all? It is not. The mind is naturally empty of essence, but it is also clear. This is the union of clarity and emptiness, and the union of wisdom and the expanse taught in the path of the sutras. This is present in the nature of the mind itself. But we have not really thought about what this means. We direct our attention outward, follow thoughts of all sorts of things, and get distracted. But all we really need to do is know what is present in the mind.

In order to know that, Khenpo Gangshar says, "Don't pursue the past." Often we remember things that happened in the past and think about them. We think, "Last year I went to that place. I had such and such a conversation. When I did this, it turned out really well. When I did that, it was bad." These and many other thoughts come up, but we should not pursue them when we are meditating. We should just be loose and relaxed and not follow the past.

Khenpo Gangshar also says, "Don't invite the future." Often we think to ourselves, "Next year I ought to do this. What should I do next month? I have to do that tomorrow. What should I do this evening?" These are all thoughts of the future. Normally we need to think about them, but not when we are meditating, so we should not welcome the future. We should put all thoughts of past or future aside.

In particular during this meditation, "Do not pursue the past" means do not think even about things that happened even just a moment ago. Do not try to remember, "What was I just thinking about? Was I just resting? Was I just stable? Was that clarity? What was it that I was just meditating on?" We should not try to think about or remember what we were just doing in our meditation in that way. Similarly, we normally understand "Don't invite the future" to mean that we should not think about future plans in general, but in this context it means not even to think about what we will do in the next moment. We do not need to think to ourselves, "Now I need to start being mindful. I need to start being aware now. Now I'm going to start being clear in my meditation." We do not need to think about anything at all—we do not think about either the past or the future. We just simply look at the mind as it is right now and rest naturally in the naked, ordinary mind.

When we say "ordinary mind," that means resting in the immediate present without trying to alter the mind in any way. Ordinary mind is not something bad that we need to make into something good. Nor is it something that is not empty that we need to make empty. That is not how it is. We do not need to take something that is not clear and make it clear. We should not try to change anything in any way. If you alter it, it is not ordinary. If you follow lots of thoughts, that is not what we mean by ordinary mind. Just rest in the nature of the mind as it is, without any thoughts that are virtuous, unvirtuous, or neutral. The way it is now is ordinary mind.

There are two different ways in which we can understand the term "ordinary mind." One way is to not take control over anything and end up following our afflictions. When a thought of anger arises, we follow it; when greed arises, we lose control of ourselves to it. Similarly, we lose control of ourselves to our pride and jealousy. Although we might think of this as our ordinary state of mind, it is not what we mean here. Here it does not mean losing control of ourselves to our negative emotions. Instead, it means that we do not need to do anything at all to the essence of the mind itself.

We do not need to alter this essence in any way. We do not have to worry about what we are thinking, what is pleasant, or what is painful. We can leave this mind as it is. If we try to alter the mind in any way, thoughts will arise. But if we do not do anything to it and let it rest easily, then it is unaltered. The Kagyu masters of the past as an instruction called this the ordinary mind, or the natural state. They called it this out of their experience. This ordinary mind itself is the dharma expanse and the essence of the buddhas: it is our buddha nature. This is exactly what the term means; this is what we need to experience and recognize.

Khenpo Gangshar calls this ordinary mind "naked." If we just have mere understanding, there is a slight gap between our mind and our understanding. When we try to investigate or analyze, it is as if the mind were covered by a sort of a membrane. But here there is nothing like that. Saying "naked" means there is no covering or anything in the way. We just rest directly in it as it is without trying to correct it or re-place it. We do not think, "Is this right? I need to make it right." We do not worry, "My meditation is bad; I've got to make it good." Without any hopes or worries, we do not try to correct it or make it right in any way. When Khenpo Gangshar says "re-place," that means that we do not try one way to settle the mind and then another. We just let it be as it naturally is, resting easily in this naked, ordinary mind.

RECOGNIZING THE EXPERIENCE
OF RESTING

What does it feel like to rest like that?

> If you rest like that, your mind-essence is clear and expansive, vivid and naked, without any concerns about thought or recollection, joy or pain. That is awareness (*rigpa*).

At this point, there is no concern about what you are thinking, what you remember, what is nice, or what is painful. You will not think, "Ah, that is what it is." You will not think, "This is empty," or "This is not empty." You will not think, "Oh, that's nice," or "Oh that's not so nice," or "That's bad." There won't be any thought of pleasure or displeasure in any way at all. This is just the natural essence of the mind. It is not something that makes us jubilantly happy, nor is it something that upsets us or makes us unhappy.

But you will see the mind-essence and it will be clear and expansive, vivid and naked. When we say "clear," this is like the clear aspect of the mind. When we talk about it being clear or luminous, sometimes we understand that as meaning some sort of a light—a blazingly bright light. But that is not what this means. It means that it can know and understand. It does not stop. We do not turn into some sort of rock. That is not what happens: there is the clear, knowing aspect of the mind. It is also expansive, which means here that the clarity is vast: we can see and know many things. Then the text says "vivid and naked." "Vivid" means that it is as if we are actually seeing—it is right there and we are really seeing it. There is no doubt whether or not this is it—it is just right there. It is naked: we are not thinking about it with logic or seeing it from far away; it is right here.

There is no veil or anything covering it at all. This is what we rest in; this is the nature of the mind.

We do not try to change anything; we rest directly in equipoise—the kusulu meditates in an uncomplicated way. The reason for resting loosely like this is that our meditation is not something that is not mentally constructed and newly made. Instead, it is just the way the mind is, unaltered. Normally we are deluded by many confused appearances, but the meditation of the kusulu should be understood as knowing the nature of the mind as it is, clearly and without mistake.

This is not just something that Khenpo Gangshar says. It is also said in *The Supreme Continuum* and *The Ornament of Clear Realization* by Maitreya as well as in *The Two Books,* the tantra of the glorious Hevajra. These works all say:

> In this there's nothing to remove
> Nor anything at all to add.
> By viewing rightness rightly and
> By seeing rightly—liberation!

There is nothing to remove. We do not need to stop or get rid of anything, thinking, "This is emptiness. This cannot be established as a thing." The nature of the mind is fine just as it is. Nor is there anything to add to the mind-essence, thinking, "That is missing. This is clarity. This is something I need to gain." If we just look at the mind-essence rightly and rest in equipoise within this nature of the mind just as it is, not following our thoughts, we will see that it is rightness. We do not need to think, "It is emptiness"—its essence is naturally empty. We do not need to think, "It is clear"—its essence is naturally clear. Resting with this mind as it is is "viewing rightness rightly." When we see that essence as it is, at that moment we will be liberated from our faults and from samsara.

This is why we just rest right in the nature of mind as it is. The dharma nature is unchanging. When the great meditators of the past meditated on it, they saw that we do not need to alter it in any way. We just need to come to thoroughly know the dharma nature as it is. When we see that, this is the mind that we call clear and expansive, vivid and awake.

When Marpa the Translator met his guru Naropa and developed experience within himself, he said:

> For instance, when a mute eats sugar cane,
> It is an inexpressible experience.

When mute people eat sugar cane, they put the cane in their mouths, they taste it, and they know what it tastes like, but if you ask them what it is like, they cannot tell you. Similarly, Marpa had an experience of realization, but when he felt it, he could not express it in any way—it was an inexpressible experience. Was it something? It was not. Was it nothing? It was not. It was indescribable. This is what Khenpo Gangshar means by saying that there is no concern about what you might be thinking, what you might remember, what is pleasant, or what is painful. Without any thoughts of good or bad or anything like that, the essence of the mind is clear and expansive, vivid and naked. You might wonder if this is a nature that we have to somehow create, but it is not. It is the nature of the mind that has been present within us from the very beginning. But up to this point, we just have not looked for it. We have not seen it because we have not looked for it. If we know how to look for it, we can know what it is like. All we need to do is look for it and see it. That is the essence of the mind.

THE KNOWING QUALITY OF MIND

As I mentioned above, there is a distinction between tranquility and insight meditation. In tranquility, there is a lot of stability but not much intelligence, whereas in insight meditation we do have intelligence. In general, there are three types of intelligence: the intelligence born of listening, that born of contemplation, and that born of meditation. The intelligence born of listening and contemplating is directed outward. It is dependent upon inference, so it is a conceptual understanding or meaning generality. It means the clarity of the mind that knows, "That's right. That's what it is." But is this the intelligence present during insight meditation? It is not. The intelligence present in meditation is the intelligence born of meditation. The difference between this and the intelligence born of listening and contemplating is that the latter is conceptual knowing that gets to the point through inference. In the intelligence born of meditation, there are not many thoughts of that kind; it is actually seeing and experiencing. It is a direct experience of the essence of the mind.

When we experience our essence, do we experience it as some sort of a thing? That is not the experience we have. Do we experience it as emptiness? We do not experience it as emptiness. It is empty — something that you cannot establish, nothing at all — but at the same time there is clarity. You could call this the aspect of wisdom. It is not just blank nothingness, it is the union of clarity and emptiness. There is clarity, but the essence of this clarity is emptiness. This is what we actually experience. If we were to think about it, we would say, "Oh, that's what mind is." Of course that would just be a thought produced by our minds; when we actually experience it, we do not have this thought. Instead, we have a feeling. This is the intelligence born of meditation that comes from directly seeing the nature of mind as it is. When we directly see the nature of mind as it is, it is not just nothingness, blankness, or darkness. Instead, we experience this intelligence and rest evenly within this experience.

What do we feel in that sort of meditation? Khenpo Gangshar's instructions say:

> At the same time, there is no thought of, "Sights and sounds are out there." Everything appears unceasingly. There is also no thought of, "The perceiver, the six types of consciousness, is within." Clear and nonconceptual awareness is unceasing.

While we are resting in meditation, we do not think about external objects such as forms, sounds, scents, tastes, and touch being out there. Are there any coarse thoughts? There are not. But does this mean that everything ceases? When we are in samadhi meditation does it mean that our eyes stop seeing things, our ears stop hearing, and our nose stops smelling? At that point, our eyes can still see forms, our ears can still hear sounds, and our nose can still smell scents, but we do not think about what they are. The mind does not stop; there is clarity. External perceived objects do not cease; they continue to occur.

In terms of the internal perceiving subject, there is not any thought that there is an internal consciousness that knows the objects. We do not conceive of the six consciousnesses. But do all the consciousnesses just stop in meditation? Does the eye consciousness stop seeing form? Does the ear consciousness stop hearing sound? Does the mind completely stop? They do not. There is a consciousness that sees visual forms. There is a consciousness that hears sounds, one that smell scents, and so forth. The consciousnesses are present. Even if they were to stop, there is still naked and clear awareness. There may not be any thoughts, but there is someone who knows, understands, and sees.

Neither the six internal perceiving consciousnesses nor the six external perceived objects stop. Whether or not we examine it in great detail, the mind does not stop. When we are seeing the nature of the mind, things still appear to us. This nonconceptual, naked awareness is unceasing, and it is also clear. There is a knowing clarity: the six consciousnesses know things clearly. They do not stop: the eye does not stop seeing form, the ear does not stop hearing sound, the nose does not stop smelling scent, the tongue does not stop tasting, the body does not stop feeling touch, and sixth, mental consciousness does not stop knowing. Knowing does not stop, and so for this reason it is clear. It is clear, but there are no coarse thoughts. We are not thinking to ourselves, "That's what it is. I see this. I hear that sound." This is awareness—naked awareness. It's like there's no veil or covering; we perceive everything as it is, unceasingly. It does not become nothingness. To make it easy to understand, I often say that we do not become rocks with no thought or awareness at all. In this way the six types of outer objects and the six consciousnesses are unceasing.

Resting within this is similar to the instruction in the "Short Vajradhara Lineage Prayer" that says, "The main practice is being undistracted, as it's taught." When meditating, the main point is to be undistracted. As the prayer says:

As ones who, whatever arises, rest simply,
Not altering, in just that fresh essence of thought,
Please bless us with practice that's free of conception.

There are still things that occur—the eye, ear, and other consciousnesses continue to happen—but whatever occurs, we rest simply within it, not changing it. We do not need to do anything to the fresh essence of thoughts. The point here is to have no fixation or grasping, which is why we ask that our meditation practice be free of conception. Generally this verse is explained to teach tranquility meditation, which it does, but the tranquility it teaches is unified with insight, so it is the same as Khenpo Gangshar's instruction.

In his shorter instructions, Khenpo Gangshar says:

Directly, whatever arises, do not change it—rest naturally.

The phrase *directly* comes out of Khenpo Gangshar's own exceptional experience, and there is a reason for saying it. These instructions are not telling us to try to do something to the nature of mind after we look for it—we should not analyze it and then chase after it. You might think to yourself, "A thought occurred." Then this leads to another thought occurring, and then another, and another. First there may be a prideful thought, then maybe an angry thought, and then more and more thoughts. This is just following them, and there is no end to that.

What we really need to do is to look directly at our thoughts. We look straight at this present mind and nurture it directly. This is in relation to the way it actually is—naked. This is why he says "directly."

Whatever occurs, look directly. If a good thought arises, look directly at it, and if a bad thought arises, look directly at it. Do not alter it. You do not need to look at it, think up the sentence, "This is emptiness," and then plaster that onto your experience. Nor do you need to say, "This is clarity," and then try to see it that way. Instead, look at the essence and see it as it is, not altering it in any way. Rest naturally in equipoise within the unaltered essence itself.

LOOKING INWARD

In one of his meditation manuals, Jamgön Kongtrul Rinpoche says that the reason we do not realize the nature of the mind is not because it is too difficult, but because it is too easy. The nature of the mind is something that we have, so we think, "It can't be that." There's nothing we need to do to it; there is nothing complicated about it. Do we not realize it because it is far away? No, it is not—rather, it is too near. It is so close to us that we already have it, but we do not realize this. For this reason we do not need to make up an essence to rest in; we rest within our own nature as it is. This is how we should meditate.

When I was young, I studied philosophy, including the middle way. Middle way texts talk a lot about different types of emptiness such as categorized emptiness, uncategorized emptiness, and so forth. When I asked my khenpo, Khenpo Lodrö Rabsal, "What is this? What does emptiness mean?" he said, "Don't think so much about the outside. Think a bit about the inside, and that will help."

"Ah," I thought. "How can you do that? How can you think about the inside?" I did not understand what he meant. I thought there was probably nothing to think about on the inside.

Then later I met Khenpo Gangshar. Everyone said, "He is a strange lama. There's something different about him. You get a different feeling from him."

I wondered what they meant. The first time I saw him, there was no different feeling. I wondered what was going on and what was going to happen. Then he first gave a pointing out of sorts. He asked, "Did you recognize anything?" but nothing happened. But as I spent some time in his presence, I had the thought, "Oh, this is it. *This* is the emptiness that Nagarjuna talked about, isn't it!" Before I had thought that emptiness was something far away, but then I came to see that emptiness is really close. This happened because of the blessings of the lama.

At that point I realized what Jamgön Kongtrul Rinpoche had meant by saying it was too near. I realized what he meant by saying it was too easy. The mind is not far away; it is within us. If you fiddle with it and alter it a lot, then it becomes fabricated. That doesn't work. The essence of the mind itself, however it may be, is just the way it is. We need to meditate by looking at it the way it is.

There are many different methods for pointing out the nature of mind through symbols and so forth. Often students gain some sort of feeling during these, but it is not very stable. But these instructions on resolving, or getting straight to meditation, are the best method to point out the nature of mind. You just get right down to the meditation. You put a lot of effort into it. You meditate. You think it over. You think about what the instructions say over and over again. Sometimes the feeling is clear, and sometimes it is unclear. But when it is unclear, you do not give up. Put effort into it and meditate, and then it will become stable. Of all the different ways to point out the nature of your mind, this is the best.

11

THE BENEFITS
OF THE KUSULU'S
MEDITATION

WHAT IS THE MAIN POINT about the resting meditation of
the kusulu? It is that we do not need to make any effort or alter
anything. Why is this? Is our mind something lousy that we need to
change into something good? It is not; we do not need to change it.
We just need to recognize that our mind is rightness. We have not yet
recognized this, so we rest in meditation so that we can recognize the
nature of the mind to be the rightness that it is.

The last chapter described the experience and feelings that arise
in our mind and told us what the clear aspect of our mind is like.
Khenpo Gangshar's text next teaches the qualities and benefits of this
meditation. What is the purpose of meditating like this? How does it
affect our body? How does it affect our speech? How does it affect our
mind? First the text discusses what happens with our body:

> While in that state, your body is left to itself without fabri-
> cation, free and easy. That is the body of all the victorious
> ones. That is the essence of the creation stage.

When we are resting in equipoise without altering anything, we
do not tighten or tense our body or try to change it in any way.
Instead, we just let it rest naturally, not doing anything to it. We let

whatever feelings happen happen. Without any discomfort at all, our body becomes free and easy. Resting in this way, we can receive all of the blessings of the creation stage.

When we see the essence of the mind, are we at that point actually doing the creation stage of visualizing a deity? We are not, but the essence of the creation stage is the realization of the nature of all phenomena as they are. That is why this practice is the essence of the creation stage and why this is the body of all the victorious ones, even though we are not doing anything in particular with our body other than just letting it rest and relax. These are the benefits for the body.

Next, the text presents the benefits for our speech:

> Your speech is free from fabrication, without efforts to track down the root of sound but simply expressing directly and openly whatever comes to mind. It is all-pervasive from the very moment of being heard, a nonarising empty resounding. That is the speech of all the victorious ones. It is the essence of all recitation.

We do not alter our speech in any way, either. We do not have any harmful intentions to say mean things or fool anyone; we just let the speech come as it is, loose and relaxed. We say whatever we need to say while experiencing the realization of the nature of the mind. While we are conversing, we do not really worry about where the sound comes from or how it occurs: the sound just happens. We hear it sound, but if we were to look for where it comes from and where it is, we would realize that at the same time as it sounds, it is empty; it just dissipates into space. While it is empty, it sounds. It is the union of sound and emptiness. Letting it be unaltered and loose, it becomes the speech of the buddhas and the essence of mantra recitation.

At this point, we are not actually reciting a mantra. However, in essence, a mantra is a way to generate the wisdom that realizes the dharma nature and the way our mind is, so resting in the nature of the mind is like the essence of that mantra recitation.

Those are the benefits for the body and speech when we are resting in the realization of the dharma nature as it is. What are the benefits for the mind? The text says:

> When you rest your mind in unfabricated naturalness, no matter what thought may arise, good or evil, happy or sad, the mind-essence, which is free from concerns about joy or sorrow, is clear and empty, naked and awake.

When we sit in samadhi, sometimes we have good thoughts. Sometimes we have bad thoughts. Sometimes we have happy thoughts, and sometimes we have unhappy thoughts. We might feel some sort of depression. Although it is possible that any of these thoughts might happen, we do not encourage the thoughts, nor do we try to repress or stop them in any way. Instead, we just go back to resting in the unfabricated naturalness just as we had been before, without altering in any way at all. If a good and joyful thought arises, there is nothing to be happy about and nothing to prolong. If you just rest loosely when a sad or harmful thought arises, there is nothing to be upset or sad about, and nothing to repress. If we just rest naturally within whatever occurs, thoughts will naturally disappear because their nature is nonarising. Thus we just let ourselves settle naturally.

If we look at the characteristics of this mind-essence that is free of concerns about joy or sorrow, it is clear and empty, naked and awake. As we said before, clear means that the mind does not become like some unknowing rock. When we say that it is empty, that means it is not some sort of inherently existent thing. But how do we look at the clear and empty mind? We look at it nakedly: we look directly without anything between the mind and ourselves. We do not investigate or alter it in any way. We look straight at it and know what its nature is. The essence of mind is also awake, which means that it is vivid and clear. It does not become some sort of dark, black unknowing, nor is there any dullness or fogginess: it is vivid and awake.

The Tibetan word for naked, *jenpa,* has another meaning as well: it also means uncooked or raw. It is like a salad: if you steam salad greens, they get limp and mushy. Frying them is not much better. So when you have salad, you eat your greens just as they are: not steamed, not fried—just raw. You don't do anything to them at all. In the same way, we do not need to think that the mind is good so we make it into something wonderful or that the mind is bad so we need to improve it. We meditate by just leaving the mind exactly as it is.

SYNONYMS FOR THE NATURE
OF THE MIND

The text continues:

> This mind-essence is the nature of all sentient beings, the realization of the buddhas of the three times, the essence of the eighty-four thousand Dharma-doors and the heart of the glorious master, the supreme guide.

Our meditation should have all four of these characteristics: clear, empty, naked, and awake. This is the nature of our own mind, and it is the same for all sentient beings — the essence of everyone's mind is the same.

The nature of the mind is also "the realization of all the buddhas of the three times." The essence of all the teachings of the Buddha, the teachings on the selflessness of the individual and on the selflessness of phenomena, is to rest in the nature of the mind. The buddhas have all taught many different types of Dharma, but they taught them all as a way to realize the nature of the mind without mistake. If you can rest in the nature of the mind, that is the realization of all the buddhas of the three times.

The Buddha taught the Dharma in order to protect all sentient beings from suffering. The Dharma that he taught is the eighty-four thousand gates of the Dharma. The eighty-four thousand gates of the Dharma are the antidotes that tame the afflictions of greed, aversion, delusion, and mixtures of those three poisons. But the root of all of these is the intelligence that realizes selflessness. All of the gates of Dharma were taught in order to generate the wisdom that realizes the selflessness of both individuals and phenomena, so the resting meditation of the kusulu is the essence of the eighty-four thousand gates of the Dharma.

It is "the heart of the glorious master, the supreme guide," which means it is the essence of the experience of the mind nature of all the masters. Many instructions say that we need to mix our minds with the mind of the master. We should have great devotion in the root and lineage masters, mix our minds with theirs, and develop excellent realization. Seeing our mind-essence is the same as doing just that.

When the Buddha taught the Dharma, he taught both the vast sutras and the profound tantras. The text next discusses how resting in the nature of mind is the essence of both of those, starting with the sutra vehicles:

> It is the transcendent knowledge of the second set of teachings and the sugata-essence of the last turning of the wheel of the Dharma.

When the Buddha taught the sutras, he taught it in what are called the three wheels of Dharma, or cycles of teachings. The first of these is the foundation vehicle, which is the basis for all the other teachings, but it is not specifically mentioned here. What is taught here are the teachings of the great vehicle from the second and third wheels of Dharma. In the second wheel of Dharma, the Buddha taught about transcendent intelligence, and in the last wheel, he taught about buddha nature.

The second wheel of Dharma teaches that all the objects that we perceive are empty and then says that the conscious subject that perceives this emptiness is transcendent intelligence, or prajñāpāramitā. When teaching emptiness directly, we follow the logic of the middle way through which we can come to understand that everything is emptiness. This is taught through the sixteen different types of emptiness or fourfold emptiness. But who is it that realizes that all phenomena are emptiness? It is the transcendent intelligence that sees the emptiness as it is and realizes it and knows it as it is. This is said to be the mother who gives birth to all of the buddhas, because if you ask where the buddhas come from, they come out of transcendent intelligence.

This transcendent intelligence is also what we are trying to come to recognize through the resting meditations of the kusulu and the analytic meditation of the pandita. The nature of all phenomena of course permeates all phenomena, but in the secret mantra vajrayana we primarily put the emphasis on our own minds. There is no need to alter the mind. With external objects, we have to stamp them with the idea that they are emptiness, but there is no need to stamp our internal mind with the idea that it is emptiness. If we know the essence of the mind itself, we will naturally realize the empty nature of how things are. The realization of the nature of the mind—the realization of the way the dharma nature actually is—is the same as what is called the great mother, transcendent intelligence, in the second wheel of Dharma.

The buddha nature taught in the third wheel of Dharma is also just that. The third wheel of Dharma primarily teaches that there is buddha nature present within the mind streams of all sentient beings. Buddha nature is the emptiness of all phenomena, but it is not inanimate emptiness. Buddha nature is the union of clarity and emptiness. The third wheel teaches that the union of the unborn empty expanse and the clear wisdom is present within the mind streams of all sentient beings. We just have not looked at that which is present within us. If we look, we can actually experience it. If we experience it and then meditate on it, then it is also called the seed of buddhahood as well as buddha nature. However, when we wander in samsara this nature of ours is concealed by the afflictions. Although we have buddha nature, we do not recognize it. We need to make it manifest by cleansing it of the stains that hide it. But what does the term buddha nature designate? It points directly to the nature of the mind. The third wheel of Dharma teaches methods to make it manifest, and in this way its meaning is just this—the nature of the mind. Thus the transcendent intelligence and buddha nature taught in the sutras are just this.

Khenpo Gangshar then discusses the tantras:

> According to the general system of mantra it is called continuity of ground, the spontaneously present mandala of the innate nature. According to the anuttara tantras it is called Guhyasamaja, Chakrasamvara, Kalachakra, and so forth.

In the mantra vehicle, there are four different classes of tantras. The first three classes—action tantra, conduct tantra, and yoga tantra—are considered lower classes in comparison to the fourth class, the unexcelled yoga tantra, so they are considered the general system of tantras. The common tantras teach about the ground tantra, path tantra, and result tantra. When we say "ground tantra," this means that now during the period when we are ordinary sentient beings there is a "continuity of the ground," our innate nature. This "spontaneously present mandala of the innate nature" is the nature of the mind-essence that we can experience in meditation.

Within the uncommon teachings of the anuttara or unexcelled tantras, there are two different traditions: the ancient Nyingma translations and the later Sarma or "new" translations. Both the Nyingma and Sarma traditions come from the lineage of the great Indian mahasiddhas, which itself came from the Buddha. The origins of the two traditions are the same, but they spread to Tibet at different times. The tantras and teachings of the ancient Nyingma school came to Tibet during the time of the great early Dharma kings, when there were many great translators who translated the tantras of the Indian tradition as well as the sutras and treatises. After the Nyingma tradition spread in Tibet, the Buddhist teachings were nearly wiped out by King Langdarma. When the Dharma was revived, once again there were many great translators who translated the Indian tantras into Tibetan. These are the translators of the new or Sarma tradition. These two traditions teach the same essential meaning, but they use different language.

In the Sarma tradition of the Kagyu and Sakya lineages, this is called the unexcelled yoga or anuttarayoga. Within the unexcelled yoga tantras, there are the father tantras such as the Guhyasamaja tantra, mother tantras such as the Chakrasamvara tantra, and nondual tantras such as the Kalachakra. The father tantras primarily teach means, the mother tantras primarily teach intelligence, and the nondual tantras teach both means and intelligence together. When we do the practices of these tantras, we meditate on the deities. Sometimes we visualize ourselves as the deity, sometimes we visualize the deities in front of us, and sometimes we visualize them inside vases, take empowerment, and so forth. But what is the foundation of all of these practices? It is the pure appearance of the essence of the mind that is naturally present within sentient beings; it is not anything else.

In the Nyingma tradition, there are three inner tantras: the mahayoga, anuyoga, and atiyoga. The mahayoga talks about the great dharmakaya, the exalted inseparability of the two truths, but this is nothing other than the nature of our mind. The anuyoga calls it "the basic mandala of the bodhichitta of the child great bliss," but it is the same thing. According to atiyoga, it is the great perfection of awareness and emptiness—dzogchen.

All of these terms are just different names given to the nature of the mind. As Khenpo Gangshar says:

> All these renowned expressions point a finger at this mind-essence itself, and nothing else.

All of the different expressions from sutras and tantras are just ways to identify and point out to us the mind-essence itself. Whether we say the emptiness of all phenomena, buddha nature, or dzogchen, they do not mean anything else. Therefore when we are practicing the resting meditation of the kusulu, we just settle our minds within this, resting within the realization of empty nature that is naturally clear. This is what the sutras teach in both the middle and final wheels of Dharma. It is also what is taught in all the tantras—the general tantras, the unexcelled yoga tantras, and the three inner tantras. These are all just different ways for us to come to know the nature of our mind—instructions that help us see it, recognize it, and then develop certainty in that recognition.

The main thing we need is to realize the nature of the mind. It should not be a fleeting realization, but should be stable and developed. Is a fleeting glimpse of the nature of mind good? Of course it is, but that alone is not enough to truly free us of the obscurations within our being. That alone cannot develop all of the wisdom within our ability. Therefore we need to have stability in our recognition. If we do, we will be able to quell all the afflictions, and as a result of this all the qualities and wisdom will naturally develop.

This is exactly what all of the Buddha's teachings of the sutras and tantras teach.

THE UNANIMITY OF TIBETAN TRADITIONS

When Buddhism spread in Tibet, there were several different traditions that developed. This happened because first a translator would go to India, learn a particular teaching, and then bring it back to Tibet and teach it. However, each translator lived in a different part of Tibet, so one translator's teachings would spread here, another's teachings would spread over there, and thus many different teachings spread. That is how the different traditions arose in Tibet. If we look at it on the most basic level, there are four great traditions of Tibet. What is the meaning that all four of these traditions teach? Do they all teach something different? They do not. All four of the different traditions of Tibet teach this very same nature of the mind. The meaning of all their teachings should be understood to be just that.

Khenpo Gangshar explains how this is the view of the Gelug school:

> This point is also presented in the Gelug school, as stated by the Great Lord (Tsongkhapa),
>
>> Appearance, the unfailing dependent origination,
>> And emptiness, understanding beyond statements—
>> As long as these two seem to be separate,
>> You have still not realized the intent of Shakyamuni.
>> When all at once and without alternation,
>> Your conviction and your notion of an object fall apart,
>> That is the moment of having completed the analysis
>>   of the view.

The basis of the view of the tradition of the mountain of Tushita, the Gelug school, is also the nature of the mind, as demonstrated by this verse from Tsongkhapa's prayer "The Three Principles of the Path." External appearances as well as the perceiving part of our mind all arise in dependence upon one another. This is the unfailing appearance of interdependence or dependent origination, which means that things happen: appearances arise unfailingly—that is, always. The essence of that is naturally empty. This emptiness is beyond the two statements, meaning that it is free of the four extremes. Here this is an understanding that we develop through logic: we come to realize that we cannot express it in words. Normally we think that when there are appearances, there can be no emptiness, and that when there is emptiness, there cannot be appearances. We think of these two as separate. Appearances are appearances. When something appears, it is true and real. It is there. Emptiness is emptiness, void and nothingness; there is nothing there. So these two must be separate, we think. But when we think of them in this ordinary way, we have not really understood. If these two seem exclusive of each other—when there are appearances there is no emptiness, and when there is emptiness there are no appearances—we have not realized "the intent of Shakyamuni," that is, what he is teaching.

Actually, when we develop intelligence through study and then meditate, we begin to see that appearance and emptiness are not separate. We see that they do not alternate: at the same time as things appear, they are empty. At the same time as they are empty, they have the capacity to appear. We can see that this is the same as the nature of our mind: the mind is clear and knowing and yet at the same time it is empty. At the same time as it is empty, it is clear and knowing. This is what we call the spontaneous presence of mind, when the conception of an object falls apart. Appearance and emptiness are understood to be the same. This is when we have fully understood the view. Realizing this is the same in essence is realizing the unity of the clarity and emptiness of the nature of the mind. This is how Tsongkhapa, the founder of the Gelug school, presented the nature of the mind, and the intent of his teaching is the same as what Khenpo Gangshar teaches.

The second of the four major schools of Tibetan Buddhism is the Sakya school. There were five main forefathers of the Sakya lineage, one of whom was the Lord of Dharma, Drakpa Gyaltsen, who was prophesied by Manjushri.

The Lord of Dharma, Drakpa Gyaltsen, has said, "When you have clinging, it is not the view." The Dharma masters of the Sakya school regard their view of undivided samsara and nirvana to be nonfixation.

Drakpa Gyaltsen talked about freedom from the four fixations. He says, "When you have clinging, it is not the view." If you cling to something as existing or as not existing, you have not seen or realized the view. The main point of the Sakya school is thus nonfixation. Thus the naked awareness that does not alter anything is the proper view. For this reason, the Sakyapa have what they call the view of the indivisibility of samsara and nirvana, which means to rest loosely, without fixation within the mind-essence, so the teachings of the Sakya school are also the same.

This is also the main teaching of the third school, the Kagyu lineage:

> Moreover, according to the matchless Kagyupa masters, glorious Rangjung Dorje proclaimed,
>
> > Everything's not true, not false,
> > Like moons in water, say the wise.
> > This ordinary mind itself
> > Is dharma expanse, the victors' essence.
>
> Thus, the luminous mahamudra is also nonfixation.

This passage Khenpo Gangshar cites is from Rangjung Dorje's "A Treatise on Buddha Nature." It means that all knowable phenomena are neither true nor false, like a reflection of the moon in water. If you see the moon in water, of course you see it, but is the moon really there? No, it is not, but you have to admit that you do see it in the water. All knowable phenomena are similarly neither true nor false. This is what the wise say, but really when we are meditating we don't need to do any of this. We do not need to say it is true. We do not need to say it is false. We don't need to say anything. What this actually points to is ordinary mind—the totally unaltered ordinary mind. It can be called the dharma expanse, or it can be called buddha nature, the essence of all the victors. Nurturing it without altering it is the luminous mahamudra that does not have any fixation or clinging. Thus the meaning of mahamudra is the same.

For this reason, Khenpo Gangshar says:

> It is said that all the learned and accomplished masters of India and Tibet had the same realization and there is not a single master who claims that the realization of the main part of practice is anything other than nonfixation. That is the meaning you should understand yourself and what you should point out to others.

When Buddhism spread, there were many learned and accomplished masters in India. When we say masters, this includes both scholars— those learned in terms of studying and contemplating—and the maha-siddhas, the people who practiced this through meditation. What they realized and taught is exactly the same as this. Since Buddhism spread to Tibet in the seventh century, there have been many learned and accomplished masters in many different traditions. There may have been many traditions, but the meaning they all taught was exactly the same. Whether you look at the words of the Buddha himself, the commentaries and treatises written by the great scholars, the meaning the great meditators meditated upon, or the teachings of the Gelug, Sakya, Kagyu, or Nyingma schools, all of them teach just this lack of fixation and the realization of the nature of the mind. None of them teach anything different. The teachings of all the Indian and Tibetan scholars and mahasiddhas all come to this one point. The actual practice of the Nyingma, Sakya, Kagyu, and Geluk lineages is all just this. What we actually practice, the foundation of our meditation, the essence of our samadhi, is nonfixation, which means resting in equipoise within the mind the way it is, not altering it.

This is also something we need to know and understand for ourselves. All of the buddhas have taught this, scholars have commented on it and explained it, and the great meditators have practiced it and given instructions on it. They did this so that we could know it thoroughly. There are two ways we can come to know it: through study and inference or by knowing it directly. The way we need to know it is through a direct yogic experience in meditation. We need to develop the discernment that knows this. This discernment is not the intelligence of either listening or contemplation; it is the intelligence of meditation.

Is just knowing it enough? It is not. The reason is that all sentient beings want to be happy. All sentient beings want to be free of suffering. Because all sentient beings want to be happy and free of suffering, we need to point this out to others—to help them see that this is the Dharma that they, too, need to know. We should help them to develop interest in this. Once they have developed interest in it, we should teach them how to practice meditation and develop samadhi within themselves. This is the meaning you should understand and what you should point out to others.

PUTTING IT INTO PRACTICE

> This completes the section that indicates that your body, speech, and mind are the Body, Speech, and Mind (of the victorious ones).

Through the instructions in this section, we can realize that our own body is the same as the body of the Buddha, that our speech is the Buddha's speech, and that our mind is the wisdom mind of the Buddha. Our body is not the second-rate heap we normally think it is, but the body of the victorious ones, the essence of the creation stage. If we realize the nature of our own mind, we will see it as just that. We might think that our speech is nothing other than the amalgamation of all the unvirtuous things we say and that it just brings us problems. But if we realize the nature of the mind, we see that it is the essence of all the mantras. We normally think that our mind is under the control of the three poisons of greed, hatred, and delusion. But if we realize the nature of the mind, we see that it is the essence of the wisdom mind of all the buddhas. This is the benefit of seeing the nature of our mind. This is pointing out that the nature of our body is the essence of the creation stage; the nature of our speech is the essence of all mantra recitation, and the nature of our mind is the essence of the mind of all the buddhas.

Whatever practice we do—whether of the creation stage, completion stage, or any other type—the essence of the practice is to rest in our dharma nature as it is, to rest in our mind as it is. It is possible that you might misunderstand this point and think that anything else is unnecessary and that all we need to do is rest in the nature of mind. You might wonder why we should even bother with all the different practices and methods, such as gathering merit through being generous and so forth. When people heard these instructions, some of them misunderstood them. They thought Khenpo Gangshar was saying that all the other practices are unnecessary or even pointless. There is even a story about one monk who destroyed his cymbals because he thought that the only thing to do was meditate on the nature of the mind! But that is a mistake. Of course if you can get straight down to meditation without any further ado, that is wonderful, but the practices of creation and completion, making offerings, and gathering merit are all helpful for your meditation. It is important to do the other practices—they are necessary and beneficial, and you should do as many of them as you can. However, the practice that fulfills the essence of all the practices is just this meditation on the nature of the mind.

What is important here is that we should not just leave it at simply knowing the nature of our mind: we need to practice it. When we practice meditating on the nature of our mind, sometimes we feel like everything is going very well and our meditation is exceptionally clear. When that happens, however, we should not be overjoyed and attached to it. We should not think how wonderful our meditation is. Other times we do not have any clear experience, but there is no need to be disappointed or depressed about that, either. There is no reason to think that we are terrible meditators or that we have lost our meditation. We should not think like that.

What we should do is maintain strong mindfulness and awareness continuously, as Takpo Tashi Namgyal says in *Clarifying the Natural State*. While we are doing our meditation practice, we should maintain strong mindfulness and awareness. Then when we get up and do all the things we do after our meditation, we must not forget our mindfulness and awareness. Whether our meditation seems good or

bad, we need to keep it up continuously with mindfulness and awareness. Many great meditators have said that a moment of confusion
can lead to a hundred confusions: you get confused once, that leads
to more confusion, which leads to more and more confusion; eventually you end up with a hundred different confusions. Or you might
have one thought, which leads to another and another, and you end
up with hundreds of thoughts. That is not what we want: we need to
rely on strong mindfulness and awareness, and that will keep us from
falling prey to confusion.

And so that is how we need to practice. We need to recognize the
nature of our mind and the nature of phenomena. Then we need to
sustain this recognition with our mindfulness and awareness. Takpo
Tashi Namgyal says this should not be a sporadic sort of mindfulness
and awareness; what we need is vast and encompassing mindfulness and awareness. If our mindfulness is sporadic, it will not really
help us. If our mindfulness and awareness are continuous, we will
develop experience, and this will help us. Therefore the way we need
to practice is to first contemplate what the nature of mind is like,
and then come to know and experience what the nature of the mind
is. Once we recognize the nature of the mind, we need to sustain
that recognition.

What is most important is to have conviction and faith in the
Dharma. You should think to yourselves that you are receiving wonderful instructions on the Dharma. You must have confidence. The
second important point is that you should just rest in equipoise without trying to do anything or alter anything.

THE NATURE OF SIGHTS, SOUNDS,
AND THOUGHTS

Khenpo Gangshar then cites a passage from Guru Rinpoche that also
teaches the nature of the mind. The passage is from *The Supplica-
tion in Seven Chapters,* a well-known prayer that teaches the essential
points of practice clearly and thoroughly, and that is frequently recited in the Nyingma tradition. Jamgön Kongtrul Lodrö Thaye found
this passage particularly profound and helpful. He had been staying

with his master Situ Pema Nyinche, but it came time for him to leave, so he went to say good-bye to Situ Pema Nyinche, who was in retreat at the time, and asked for some instructions. Situ Pema Nyinche taught him this passage, which points out the nature of the body, speech, and mind, just once. Because of these instructions, Jamgön Kongtrul was able to realize the nature of his mind, as related in his life story.

These powerful words bring great blessings. They describe how all the external objects—forms and sounds we perceive outside ourselves—and all the thoughts that arise in our mind are aspects of our body, speech, and mind, and point out their nature. First he teaches that all that appears to our eyes is the body of the deity:

> Thus all the things that appear to your eyes,
> The outer and inner, the world and its inhabitants,
> Appear, so rest in the essence that has no self-clinging.
> Perceiver and perceived purified, the clear and empty
>   body of the deity.
> I supplicate the lama who is naturally liberated desire.
> I supplicate Uddiyana Padmasambhava.

When we look out, we see colors, shapes, mountains, and so forth. We see the environment of the outer world and its inhabitants. The environment we see includes all the mountains, valleys, rivers, forests, and so forth, and the inhabitants are the various different types of beings we see—people, fish, birds, and all the other sorts of animals and beings. When we see the environment and its inhabitants, of course they do appear, but we should "rest in the essence that has no self-clinging." We should not think of them as being real things and cling to them. We should not think of them as being good or bad. We should not think they are something inherently real. We should not think they are nothing and emptiness. Instead, we should just rest within the unaltered mind itself without holding on to anything. If we just rest within the mind, the perceiver—our mind—and the perceived—external objects—are purified. There is nothing impure at all. We see them, but there is no clinging or attachment, so clarity and emptiness are brought together and all we see becomes the body of the deity. It may not actually appear as the deity's body, but it is the essence of the deity's body. This is the same point Khenpo Gangshar discussed above about the body: not altering the body is the essence of the creation stage. If we can recognize this, it is "the clear and empty body of the deity." In this state we have no clinging or attachment to the world or its inhabitants; although they naturally appear, we rest in meditation without fixation, so we "supplicate the lama who is naturally liberated desire." We supplicate Uddiyana Padmasambhava, or Guru Rinpoche, so that we can be free of all attachment and realize the nonexistence of the perceiver and perceived. This is liberating our own body as the body of the deity.

The prayer goes on to address the aspect of speech:

> Thus all the sounds that resound in your ears,
> To which you cling as pleasant or unpleasant,
> Sound emptily, so rest in the nature with no thinking.
> Empty resounding, the Buddha's speech with no arising
>   or ceasing.
> I supplicate the empty resounding Victors' speech.
> I supplicate Uddiyana Padmasambhava.

When we hear with our ears, we hear various different sounds. Some of them are pleasant, such as beautiful melodies. But sometimes we hear unpleasant sounds, such as ugly tunes that we do not like. When we hear words, they may not have a melody, but in terms of meaning, they may be harsh and unpleasant, or their meaning may sometimes be attractive and pleasing. In this way, we cling to the many different sounds that we hear as pleasant or unpleasant, but in actuality they "sound emptily, so rest in the nature with no thinking." This means that although they sound and we can hear them, we cannot prove their nature to be anything. Therefore if they are pleasant, we should not cling to them, thinking they are nice. If they are harsh and unpleasant, we should not feel aversion to them, thinking they are bad. Thus they are just empty resounding: we hear them, but they are empty of any essence. Because they are empty, in their essence they neither arise nor cease, like the speech of all the buddhas.

But even though they are empty, they resound; at the same time as they resound, they are empty. When we can see that nature, that is the essence of the speech of all the buddhas.

Next is the mind and mental perceptions:

> Thus all the thoughts that move before the mind,
> The afflictions, the five poisons, whatever occurs,
> Don't need to be anticipated, analyzed, or altered.
> By letting their motion alone, you are freed into the
> Dharmakaya.
> I supplicate the lama of self-liberated awareness.
> I supplicate Uddiyana Padmasambhava.

We have many different thoughts that occur as the objects of our mental consciousness. Sometimes they are good thoughts, and sometimes they are thoughts motivated by the afflictions, the five poisons. When the Buddha called the afflictions poisons, this was a skillful way to tell us that they must be given up. The five poisons are the afflictions of greed, aversion, delusion, jealousy, and pride. When one of these arises, we should not think of it as good and follow it. But we should not think of it as bad or as something we need to stop and alter or get rid of either. We should not engage the afflictions by anticipating: we do not need to think, "This going to happen. I'm going to feel desire in a moment." Nor do we need to constantly analyze and rehash all of our thoughts. We do not need to change them in any way or try to make bad thoughts good. Instead, we should just let them alone. If we just let the motion of the mind settle, then it naturally stops because its nature is emptiness. This is the naturally self-liberated awareness, the nature of our mind. Because it is empty by nature and cannot be established as anything, it is freed into the dharmakaya.

The nature of our mind is awareness, and awareness is naturally liberated. We do not need to do anything to it. We do not need to think of it as something to take up that we need to get more of, nor do we need to think of it as something bad to be blocked or suppressed. We should understand that it is naturally liberated. These are instructions on using what appears to our mind for our samadhi.

The next verse summarizes how our bodies, speech, and minds are naturally empty:

> The purity of what is perceived outside—the appearance
>   of the object,
> The liberation of what perceives from the inside—the
>   mind-essence,
> And the clear radiance between: within the recognition
>   of this,
> May the compassion of the sugatas of the three times
> Liberate the mind streams of those who are like me.

In terms of outside appearances, there are perceived objects. They do appear, but their appearance is pure—they are naturally empty of essence. If we realize that they are naturally empty and pure, there is no way external objects can harm us because their essence is empty. In terms of what is inside, there is our perceiving mind, but that, too, cannot be established and is empty of essence. For that reason, it is naturally free of thoughts and afflictions. Thus the mind-essence is naturally liberated. Between the internal perceiving mind and the external perceived object there is clarity, which is the luminosity or clear radiance of the mind. That is neither the external object nor the internal mind. This clear radiance is the nature of our mind, and we need to recognize it.

External objects and the internal perceiving mind are both naturally pure and naturally empty. But even though they are empty, there is not just an inanimate, blank void. They are clear: by their very nature, they can manifest as qualities and wisdom. The prayer is that when we recognize this clear radiance and these natures, the compassion and blessings of all the buddhas of the three times bring us to liberation where we have no clinging or attachment. This is what it means to recognize the Buddha's body, speech, and mind. Our bodies are the bodies of the all the buddhas; our speech is the speech of the buddhas; our minds are the wisdom mind of the buddhas' dharmakaya. If we can realize the way that these are, we will be liberated immediately.

The great treatise *The Supreme Continuum* says that buddha nature is present within the mind streams of all sentient beings. We all have the nature of the mind, but not all sentient beings can experience or recognize it. This is taught through nine analogies, including the analogy of a statue of a buddha hidden in a lotus flower. One of the analogies is of a large piece of gold that falls to the ground and over the course of hundreds and thousands of years is covered by dirt, litter, and filth. The essence of the gold itself does not change in any way, but it is no longer particularly useful. Later a poor man comes and builds a shack on top of the gold. He leads an impoverished, miserable life full of suffering, but actually, there is no need for that—there is a huge piece of gold right below his house. But the gold does not help him in any way.

Then a clairvoyant person comes along and sees how difficult and miserable a life the poor man leads. But he also sees that it does not have to be like that. If the poor man just dug a bit beneath his shack, he would find the gold, which he could use to end his suffering. So the clairvoyant tells the poor man that there is gold and that he can use it. If there were no gold, the clairvoyant person could not help the poor man. But the gold is there. Even though the gold is there, if the clairvoyant person did not point it out, there would be no way to use it. Both of these conditions must be fulfilled.

As in this analogy, the nature of our mind is the cause for us to rid ourselves of all the afflictions and develop all the qualities of realization. It is present within all sentient beings, but like the poor man we do not know it is there. Because we do not know it is there, we fall under the control of the afflictions of greed, aversion, delusion, pride, jealousy, and so forth. We experience the different types of suffering of the six realms of wandering beings. We encounter many difficulties and obstacles and are unable to achieve liberation and omniscience. Actually, there is no need for us to suffer. All of us sentient beings have what is called buddha nature in the great treatise *The Supreme Continuum* and called the nature of the mind in these instructions. We have it, but we do not know that we have it.

Like the clairvoyant person, the complete and perfect Buddha first taught that buddha nature is present within the mind streams of all sentient beings. This teaching was passed down through all the lineage lamas to our root lama, who points the nature of mind out to us. If we put effort into it, understand it, and know it, we will gradually be able to free ourselves from the afflictions that must be abandoned. We will gradually develop the qualities and wisdom that must be realized. As a result of this, we will no longer experience the suffering of samsara and the lower realms. This is why we need to know that our mind is not far away—it is close. Its nature has been present from beginningless time. Gold can be buried for hundreds or thousands of years, but its essence never changes. In the same way, the essence of our mind or buddha nature never changes. It is right there for us to know.

12

DISTINGUISHING MIND
AND AWARENESS

THE RESTING MEDITATION of a kusulu is like the essence of all the traditions of Dharma. It is the essence of the great seal, the great perfection, path and result, and emptiness. It is necessary to receive these instructions, but once you have received them, what should you do with them? There is a danger of what we call not taking care of your meditation. If you receive the instructions and start meditating but then do not keep it up, you will lose your meditation and revert back to your old bad habits. When you receive such experiential meditation instructions, you absolutely must practice them.

In terms of how to practice them, the three forefathers of the Kagyu lineage—Marpa the Translator, Milarepa, and Gampopa—provide examples of different ways in which we can practice. They all led different lifestyles in different situations, and so they serve as examples of the different ways that students can live and practice Dharma according to their own needs and inclinations.

Lord Gampopa Youthful Moonlight, for example, led the life of a fully ordained monk. He took monastic vows, built a large temple, and took care of a large sangha while at the same time managing to maintain his practice of mahamudra and meditation on the nature of the mind-essence. By doing so, he was able to achieve a state of great accomplishment, demonstrating that we, too, can achieve this state if we lead a monastic life. This path is beneficial for those people who have the inclination to fully renounce the worldly life: it provides a good opportunity to practice the Dharma.

But many Dharma students are not able to become monastics, and they might wonder whether they can practice the Dharma without becoming a monk or a nun. There is no one who says that you can't practice the Dharma if you don't take vows. For example, the great yogi Milarepa was not a monk, but he practiced the Dharma very intensely. He led an uncomplicated and austere life. He did not worry about food, clothing, money, or a place to stay. He did not have even a whit of attachment to this life. If he had food while he practiced meditation, that was fine. If he did not have food, that also was fine. If he had clothing, that was fine, and if he did not have clothing, that also was fine—he practiced diligently regardless of external circumstances in caves and other remote places, and he became a great mahasiddha. If you have the fortune and ability to practice like Milarepa, that is wonderful. If you do not have the fortune or ability to do it to the extent that Milarepa did but can do even a little bit, that is also wonderful.

Not everyone has the opportunity to practice in such a way, but no one says that you cannot practice the Dharma and achieve results if you do not practice exactly like Milarepa. Whatever lifestyle you lead, you can still practice Dharma. Marpa the Translator, for example, led an entirely different life. He had a wife and children, wealth and possessions. He enjoyed those, but at the same time he was diligent about his Dharma practice. He first studied and contemplated the Dharma, and then practiced it. Through his practice he achieved the great accomplishments of the Dharma. He is like the spring from which all of our Kagyu teachings flow.

Like Marpa the Translator, you probably live in a household and have a certain amount of wealth, but you can still practice the Dharma. If you can practice like Marpa and attain such a high degree of realization, then that is extremely fortunate. Even if you cannot attain such a high degree of realization, any amount of Dharma practice you do will still be beneficial. Whether you take Marpa, Milarepa, or Gampopa as your model, you can practice the Dharma.

The great masters of ancient India, the eighty-four mahasiddhas, also provide many different examples of different lifestyles. The mahasiddhas came from all walks of life: they were male and female masters who practiced the Dharma in ways that fit with their lifestyles and managed to achieve great accomplishments. Among them was King Indrabhuti, who was a powerful king. He had a large kingdom over which he reigned, and therefore had great responsibilities. He was also extremely wealthy and had many sensory pleasures to enjoy. But he was not led astray by his pleasures and wealth, nor was he overwhelmed by his responsibilities. He was able to do his practice while keeping up his responsibilities and attained realization in this way.

Like King Indrabhuti, you might have great wealth and resources. Sometimes you might wonder to yourself whether you have to give it all up in order to practice Dharma. That is not necessary. If you wish to give up your wealth, that is fine, but if you do not, you can still practice the Dharma and achieve results.

The great pandita Nagarjuna provides yet another example. Nagarjuna was learned and wise, and knew the philosophies of both Buddhist and non-Buddhist schools. He also was extremely intelligent and proved his points through sharp and penetrating logic. He composed many original treatises, which were so influential that they mark a turning point in both Buddhist and non-Buddhist philosophy. The logic and reasoning in Nagarjuna's profound treatises on emptiness were so overpowering that Buddhists were compelled to accept his positions, and there is even said to be a marked difference between the treatises written by non-Buddhist philosophers who appeared before Nagarjuna and those who came after him. His logic was so persuasive that they were forced to change the positions they held in their own philosophical schools. In his treatises, he refuted many incorrect positions and established a new tradition of scholarship. But he was not merely a scholar who only took a scholastic interest and never practiced, distracted by his intellectual pursuits. Because of his realization of the profound nature of emptiness, he was both a great scholar and a mahasiddha. Similarly, there are many people today who are scholars, such as professors. The example of

Nagarjuna shows that you can pursue scholarly work and practice meditation at the same time.

Another example is someone who was neither a great scholar nor wealthy or powerful in any way, and who led a very simple life. This is the great mahasiddha Tilopa. He supported himself by pounding sesame seeds to extract the oil. Externally, he made the efforts of grinding sesame seeds, and internally, at the same time, he practiced mahamudra, through which he attained great accomplishments. You might wonder whether you could lead such a simple life and practice the Dharma, and the example of Tilopa shows that you can. You can live and practice like Tilopa and also achieve the ultimate result.

Whatever our lifestyle may be, we need to practice the Dharma. But how do we actually fit the practice into our lives? In general, there are two parts to Dharma practice: the actual practice of resting in equipoise, and postmeditation practice. The actual practice of meditation involves requesting teachings from a master, developing faith and devotion, and then doing either the analytic meditation of the pandita or the resting meditation of the kusulu. When we have not yet discovered the nature of our mind and are unable to experience its essence, we should practice the analytic meditation of the pandita. When we have progressed through this preliminary of an analytic meditation and our minds are mostly able to rest in equipoise, we do not need to always look for where our mind is or what its essence is. At some point you start having some experience, and that is when you should do the resting meditation of the kusulu. If you are able to rest within that meditation, that is good, but if not you can return to the analytic meditation for a while. Once your meditation progresses and you are able to simply rest, then you should just sustain the resting meditation of the kusulu.

We need to do both of these practices, but that alone is not enough. We also need to practice in our postmeditation activities. Whenever we get up from meditation, we do things. We might eat, sleep, go someplace, or do any number of things. The time when we are doing all these things other than meditation is what we call postmeditation. The most important thing to do in postmeditation is to not forget the experience of meditation, resting in equipoise. We should try to maintain our mindfulness and awareness. If we can do that, our postmeditation will enhance our actual meditation practice, and our meditation practice will enhance our postmeditation practice. Our equipoise will grow clearer and more stable and we will also have somewhat fewer difficulties in postmeditation. Of course we still have to see people, have conversations, and do our jobs in postmeditation, and it is possible that there will be worries and problems. But when problems occur, we shouldn't give up. We must be able to remember the essence of our meditation practice, and once we remember it we need to think about it. If we practice both meditation and postmeditation in this way, things will get clearer and better. Khenpo Gangshar said that this is the essence of his instructions on simple and uncomplicated practice.

THE PROBLEM WITH DISTRACTION

At this point we need to be able to know whether our meditation is going well or badly. In order to be able to know that, we need to know whether we are distracted or not, and so in his shorter instructions Khenpo Gangshar says that we need to distinguish between being distracted and not being distracted. Sometimes when we are meditating on the nature of the mind, we get a little distracted, but other times we can rest without distraction. We need to be able to clearly differentiate these two situations. Khenpo Gangshar continues,

> If you are undistracted and natural, there can be neither help nor harm. This is awareness.

If we can eliminate distraction and rest naturally undistracted with the naked and direct experience of the essence of the mind, nothing can either help or harm us: if something good happens we will not get attached to it so it cannot really help us. If someone does something bad to us we will not feel any anger over it, so it cannot really harm us. This is what it means to say that there is neither help nor harm.

In dzogchen, this is called distinguishing between mind and awareness. Being undistracted and resting naturally is what we call awareness. Being distracted by thoughts is what we call mind. When we say distinguishing, what we mean is that we need to know whether our meditation is good or not. This comes down to mind and awareness, so we need to be able to distinguish between these two. As Khenpo Gangshar says:

> It is very important to distinguish the difference between mind and awareness.

Sometimes we look at the nature of the mind, recognize it, and rest within it. That is called awareness. But sometimes we forget what we're doing and many different thoughts arise. These thoughts well up because of the imprints of habituation from beginningless time. When we are unable to rest in equipoise and there is some confusion, or when we forget what we are doing, that is mind. These are the two aspects we need to differentiate. If we confuse them, there is a danger that we will mistake not meditating for meditating and our practice will not go well. We need to clearly distinguish what is meditation and what is not meditation. When are we distracted and not meditating? When are we undistracted and meditating? Clearly knowing the difference between these two is very important.

The reason this is so important is as the Great Omniscient One, Longchenpa, described:

> The big oxen pretending to know ati nowadays
> Claim that discursive thinking is awakened mind.
> Such ignorant people, in their realm of darkness,
> Are far away from the meaning of the natural Great
> Perfection.

Although many people think they are practicing atiyoga or dzogchen, many of them do not know how to differentiate between mind and awareness. Such people are actually just big, stupid oxen— bullheaded and dumb. If they try to meditate, they don't know how. They don't know what is good and what is bad. When such people practice dzogchen, a thought happens and then they follow it, thinking that the movement of thoughts in the mind is all ultimate bodhichitta. They think it is the dharma nature, the way the mind-essence is: they think they have realized the nature of all phenomena. But this is a big mistake. Actually, all of these discursive thoughts circling through their minds are the confused appearances of samsara, not ultimate bodhichitta, and to think they are wisdom or ultimate bodhichitta is actually complete delusion. People who think they are in the midst of darkness. They lack clarity. If they could come to a place where it was clear and light, they would be able to see and to free themselves, but they do not know this and instead wander about in the confused darkness of delusion. This is why they are said to be far away from the natural great perfection—they are unable to practice dzogchen meditation.

This is the difficulty that can arise if we do not distinguish between mind and awareness—between the distracted and undistracted mind. In addition to recognizing the nature of the mind, we also need to know when we are experiencing resting in awareness of the nature of mind and when we are experiencing mind, the confused aspect.

The reason we need to distinguish mind from awareness is that there is a nondistracted aspect that recognizes the nature of mind and a distracted aspect that has forgotten its nature. When we rest within the nature of mind, that is what Khenpo Gangshar calls "the continuity of undistracted naturalness," but when we get distracted, we forget that experience and lose it. Then many thoughts arise and the mind becomes unclear. It is as if we don't know when we got distracted. In some meditation manuals, this is called the undercurrent. There are small thoughts that start without us knowing how or when. This distracted aspect is called mind. The undistracted mind that has mindfulness and attentiveness—the continuity of undistracted naturalness—is called awareness.

Above we used the word *mind* when discussing looking at the nature of mind, and here we are using *mind* for the distracted aspect that must be given up. Although the word is the same, the meaning is different. In this context, mind is when experience has not yet arisen within ourselves, or if experience has arisen, it is when we fall under the control of thoughts. Above, looking at the nature of the mind means recognizing the mind itself and knowing its utterly pure nature. We need to realize that these are different. Resting in equipoise undistracted within the recognition of the nature of the mind is what we call awareness.

To put it concisely, awareness is unconfused—it is what realizes the nature of things. When we have confusion or thinking, that is mind. We need to clearly differentiate these two because, as Khenpo Gangshar says:

> If you fail to distinguish between mind and awareness you may engage in conduct which confuses cause and result and thus turn away from the path in which view and conduct are united.

Sometimes our awareness is very strong and clear, and at such times there is no danger of mixing up karma, cause, and effect. But sometimes when we do not clearly distinguish the confusion of mind from awareness, we might think that the distracted aspect of mind is meditation. Many thoughts will arise, and we will not deal with them, thinking that this is dzogchen. If that happens, the afflictions will arise, we will follow them, and then we will engage in wrongdoing. We will have turned away from the path in which view and conduct are united. We will disregard karma, cause, and effect. We will not give up nonvirtue and will not cultivate virtue. We will confuse cause and effect, and make many mistakes. When we have the right view and understand the difference between mind and awareness, this leads us to good behavior—proper view and proper conduct are united. But if we do not distinguish between them and do not behave well, it is the opposite: our view and conduct will not be good.

When we meditate on the nature of the mind, we need to have both right view and right conduct. It is very important that we achieve a proper understanding of the view and that we realize the mind-essence. At the same time, our conduct should be proper; it should not be mixed with misdeeds, obscurations, and nonvirtue. When our view and conduct are united, our good view enhances our conduct, and our conduct enhances the view. When we are meditating, we need to follow this unified path, but if we are not able to differentiate mind from awareness, we will turn away from the path.

RECOGNIZING AWARENESS, IDENTIFYING MIND

We need to differentiate mind from awareness, but what is mind? What is awareness? Khenpo Gangshar explains:

> When experiencing the continuity of undistracted naturalness, awareness is free from a reference point, like sky, without even a speck of joy or sorrow, hope or fear, benefit or harm, whether you meet with positive or negative conditions.

Awareness is when our mind is undistracted—when we recognize the nature of our mind as it is and realize its essence. In the instructions on mahamudra, we say that we need to have mindfulness and attentiveness and not let our mind become distracted. When we call this naturalness, that means that we are resting in the nature of how things are: it is seeing the nature of mind. When we see the nature of mind, what feelings do we have? We might meet at some point with positive conditions when everything is going well and things are nice and pleasant, but we do not feel any joy, any great hope, or any clinging. We might meet with negative conditions—things might go badly, we might feel pain and suffering, or encounter difficulties and things we do not like. But we do not feel any anger or aversion toward these things.

When we are resting in this samadhi, if positive conditions arise we do not think to ourselves, "That's good," and feel happy. Likewise, if negative conditions arise, we do not think, "That's bad," and get depressed. We have neither joy nor displeasure. If we were to feel joy or pleasure when meeting with positive conditions, we would feel a lot of hope, and if we felt sad or depressed about negative conditions, we would become fearful. But when resting in equipoise within the natural state, there is neither any hope nor any fear. When we say "hope or fear," hope is thinking, "I hope things turn out well in the future" and fear is thinking, "I'm afraid that in the future things are going to go badly." But here there is not even a trace of either of these feelings.

Everything is the same, tranquil and peaceful, and we rest within this state. When we encounter good situations, they cannot really benefit us in that they do not make us happy or give us any hope. When we encounter bad situations, they do not harm us in that they do not make us fearful or give us any problems. We do not have any of the difficulties that arise from hope and fear; we don't have any clinging or attachment. It is like the sky or space, without even a speck of joy or sorrow, hope or fear, benefit or harm. There is no clinging and no fear at all. This is what the awareness is—a very clear and stable state during meditation in which we experience radiant, blissful emptiness.

Well then, what is mind?

> The character of (dualistic) mind is evident the moment you get slightly distracted and encounter (the same) conditions and you feel joy or sorrow. Having given rise to joy or sorrow, you will accumulate karmic actions.

We try to rest undistracted within the experience of the nature of the mind, but we have old habits and sometimes do get slightly distracted. This means that we have lost our mindfulness and attentiveness. In dzogchen, this is called mind, and in mahamudra it is said that our mindfulness is not stable. When we get slightly distracted, thoughts can arise in our mind, some of which will be of like or dislike, and we will then forget to rest in naturalness. Our mind gets distracted and confused. If we encounter a good situation, we feel happy and joyful. We think, "How nice! I like that! I want that!" and we then feel attached. Because of that, we perform an action and accumulate karma. If we encounter a bad situation, we think, "How horrid! Get that away from me," and feel aversion or jealousy, which also leads us to act. Once we feel either attachment or aversion, we will commit good or bad actions and accumulate karma. This then causes us to wander in samsara—once we accumulate karma, we will inevitably wander in samsara. Such distraction is mind.

This is how we identify mind and awareness. Awareness is nondistraction imbued with mindfulness and attentiveness. If mindfulness and attentiveness are absent, that is mind. Khenpo Gangshar gives an example:

> For example, mind is like the clouds gathering in the sky. Therefore, you must gain stability in awareness, which is like a cloudless sky. You must be able to purify the aspect of mind that is like the clouds in the sky.
>
> Through this you will be able to separate mind and awareness.

When the sky is cloudy, it is hidden and you cannot see it clearly. Similarly, when we encounter a situation, we have feelings of joy or sorrow, and as a result of this we experience attachment and aversion. But our internal awareness is like an utterly clear blue sky without a trace of a cloud. The absence of mind is called awareness. At first our awareness is not stable—sometimes it is there and sometimes it is not. We need to gain stability in this awareness, which means that we need to be able to sustain it. In order to do that, we need to purify the mind: just as a strong wind will blow away all the clouds in the sky, we need to use the strength of samadhi to purify ourselves of the clouds of mind so that we can see the awareness—it should be crystal clear. When we have mind, there is distraction. But if we have mindfulness, we realize that we were distracted, and the distraction immediately disappears. Once mind has been stabilized, awareness arises.

The main point is that we must be able to maintain our experience and realization. We need to be able to get rid of the problems in our meditation. In order to do that we need to know what mind and awareness are and identify them clearly. We need to make sure we are not overcome by mind and be able to rest evenly within our awareness. We need to dispel our thoughts, the clouds gathering in the sky; we need to dispel the distraction of mind and make our awareness clear like the utterly pure sky.

Some dzogchen practitioners say that mahamudra lacks these instructions on differentiating between mind and awareness and consider this to be a deficiency in mahamudra. But this is not actually the case. Although masters of mahamudra do not teach it using the same words, they do teach the same point. In *Clarifying the Natural State*, Takpo Tashi Namgyal says that when we are practicing meditation, we need to have clear and strong mindfulness and attentiveness. This actually means the same thing as differentiating mind and awareness. The way we determine whether we are distracted or not is through our mindfulness and attentiveness. Takpo Tashi Namgyal says from his own experience that this mindfulness should be clear and strong so that we immediately know if our meditation is good. Our mindfulness must have a certain strength and force to it. If our mindfulness is too lax, it is easy to become distracted. Thus the teachings on dzogchen and mahamudra are really making the same point, albeit with different words.

The reason it is the same is that when we discuss differentiating mind and awareness, we are looking at the object of the meditation and saying, "This is mind" or "This is awareness." When we say that we need strong and clear mindfulness and attentiveness, then we are looking at the perceiving subject with mindfulness and attentiveness to see whether it is confused or not. This is a way of distinguishing between mind and awareness. When we have strong and clear mindfulness and awareness, we are able to purify our minds and clarify our awareness. In this way, although the mahamudra instructions do not actually say the words "distinguishing mind and awareness," they do teach the meaning, so there is no deficiency.

There are also some manuals that say mindfulness and attentiveness are distraction and are therefore not all that good. But in order to be undistracted, you absolutely must have mindfulness and attentiveness. Takpo Tashi Namgyal also says that our mindfulness and attentiveness should not be too fussy, to put it in colloquial language; we should not be constantly fiddling with our meditation. Instead, we should maintain our experience in a spacious way. If we think, "I need to be mindful!" that is too tight. But if we look from afar in a relaxed way, then our mindfulness will be supple and spacious. Our mind should be able to rest without distraction in mindfulness. Always fiddling and being fussy does not really help much.

This concludes the teachings on the actual practice of the resting meditation of the kusulu, which began with the instructions on resolving, followed by these instructions on distinguishing. The instructions on resting meditation tell us that we are able to look at our mind. When we look, we can see and then realize its nature. Then we need to be able to sustain that: we need to maintain our practice. In order to do that, we need to distinguish between mind and awareness. Thus we must be able to purify mind and strengthen and clarify awareness. The nature of our mind is not something that we make or that someone else gives to us. The nature of mind is already present within and is something that we can recognize and meditate on. We don't need to make something that's not resting rest. We don't need to make something moving stay still. The resting meditation is just to rest in meditation within that which we already have, relaxing without altering it in any way. It is important that we nurture this continually.

PART FOUR
FOLLOWING
THROUGH IN
OUR LIVES

WHEN WE HAVE REALIZED THE NATURE OF THE MIND AS IT is, how can we use that realization to take the situations we encounter as the path and help ourselves in our human lives? Sometimes we experience disturbing emotions and the afflictions, and when that happens, how should we use our practice? When we get sick, how should we use our practice? When we come to the time of death, how can we bring our practice to really bear upon the important points? The instructions that tell us what to do in these situations are the follow-through instructions on taking situations as the path.

The follow-through instructions on taking situations as the path are extremely important. We will encounter many situations both happy and sad, and when we do, we need to be able to make our practice help us. If we can do this, it is very beneficial. Marpa the Translator called this mixing—mixing joy and suffering with our practice.

Here we call it taking situations as the path. This means that whatever we encounter, we need to be able to take it as our path. When bad things happen to us and we encounter difficulties and problems, we need to use them as a way to strengthen our experience and realization. When good things happen, we need them to increase our experience and realization. We also need to avoid being overcome by our afflictions and difficulties.

Khenpo Gangshar's instructions describe four different applications. First he describes taking joy and sorrow as the path; second, taking sickness as the path; third, taking the afflictions as the path; and lastly, taking the bardo and sleep as the path.

13

TAKING THE SITUATIONS OF OUR LIVES AS THE PATH

W E NEED TO TAKE ALL the problems we encounter as the path so that they do not really hurt us in this life. What is the method for doing this? The principal method is to maintain the experience of the nature of the mind so that they will be unable to harm us. This is something we need to be able to do. Khenpo Gangshar writes:

> The third part explains the profound advice on the subsequent application, which is based on the oral instructions that reveal direct self-liberation.

Self-liberation refers to what we discussed above in the context of Wangchuk Dorje's *Ocean of Certainty:* appearances are mind, mind is empty, emptiness is spontaneous presence, and spontaneous presence is self-liberation. Here we are discussing the natural liberation of all thoughts: when a thought arises and we recognize its nature, it is naturally liberated.

Khenpo Gangshar explains the reason for taking things as the path as follows:

> While you remain in undistracted naturalness it is utterly impossible to accumulate karma and you have cut the

stream of the further accumulation of karma. Although you are not accumulating (new) karma, do not get the idea that there is neither good nor evil to be experienced as (past) karma ripens.

When you rest undistracted within the realization of the nature of your mind, whether during the equipoise of meditation practice or during postmeditation practice, you cannot accumulate new good or bad karma because you are not experiencing any clinging or any aversion. Because you do not have any clinging, aversion, or other afflictions, you do not perform any actions with karmic consequences, and so you will no longer accumulate new karma. As Nagarjuna said,

> Desire, aversion, and delusion—
> These three produce unvirtuous acts.
> Nongreed, nonhatred, nondelusion—
> The acts that these produce are virtuous.

If desire, aversion, or delusion arise in the mind, then we will naturally accumulate unvirtuous karma. But when we have experience and realization, there is none of that, so it is impossible to accumulate karma.

When we practice dzogchen or mahamudra, there is no more karma. You might think this means that you will never be affected by the ripening of karma again, but that is not how it is: "Do not get the idea that there is neither good nor evil to be experienced as past karma does ripen." The fact that we are not accumulating new karma means that we are not creating new causes for rebirth in samsara and the lower realms, but that does not mean that we will not experience the results of the actions we have already performed.

Or you might think that now you can perform actions and accumulate karma without being affected by their ripening. But saying there is no more karma does not mean that we can do things, accumulate karma, and then just rest within the nature of the mind and not experience any consequences. It does not work like that. We cannot commit an unvirtuous act and then think, "Since I have realized the nature of my mind, I won't experience the karmic results of this act." We are not freed from virtue and nonvirtue. What it means instead is that because of our realization we do not accumulate new karma, but past karma will ripen upon us. We will experience the results of the good and bad acts we have done in the past. That is why we need to purify our karma:

> That is, unless you purify all the karmic deeds you have previously accumulated through confession, purification, and so forth, they will ripen without fail. The ripening of karma is still possible.

In the past, we had not yet realized the nature of mind, because of which we accumulated karma. This karma will definitely ripen upon us. Therefore we need to purify our misdeeds by confessing them or by accumulating merit, the strength of which will purify our misdeeds. We can eliminate our misdeeds and afflictions through either of these methods, but unless we purify our karma through them, they will ripen without fail. We should not doubt this. The full ripening of our karma will happen. Our virtuous acts will bring us pleasant results; unvirtuous or negative acts will bring us painful results. Although we do not accumulate new karma when we have attained the realization of the nature of mind, we still experience the ripening of past karma. Since we will definitely experience the ripening of unpurified karma, we need instructions to help us deal with it. That is why Khenpo Gangshar gave these instructions on taking situations as the path.

When the results of our karma ripen, how will we experience them? Karma ripens either upon our bodies or upon our mind. As Khenpo Gangshar says:

> This ripening will manifest in your body or mind and nowhere else. When it ripens in your body you will fall sick. When it ripens in your mind you will feel joy or sorrow and the thoughts of the six types of disturbing emotions will arise.

Our karmic actions do not ripen on objects outside ourselves—the earth, mountains, rocks, or anything else. They do not ripen in any other realm or any other place. They do not ripen upon our friends or relatives. They do not ripen on anyone who did not perform the act. The acts we perform will only ripen on us—on our own bodies and minds.

When our actions ripen on our bodies, we experience the results of unvirtuous acts as sickness, pain, or some other sort of physical discomfort. We experience the results of defiled virtue as pleasurable feelings or comfort. Defiled virtuous karma means the virtuous actions that we perform either at times when we do not recognize the nature of the mind or at times when we do not have the motivation of bodhichitta. These are virtuous acts that bring about temporary results. We do these actions out of a kind heart and they do bring a happy result, but that happy result is a good rebirth in this world—within samsara.

When our actions ripen on our mind, we might feel joy or sorrow. If the action was defiled virtue, we experience its result as mental pleasure or happiness. If it was an unvirtuous act, it will ripen as suffering, unpleasantness, or mental pain. Therefore defiled good actions lead to comfort and pleasure in our body and mind; unvirtuous acts bring pain, illness, and discomfort. This is how it works.

Therefore much of the joy, suffering, and illness that we experience is the result of our past karmic actions. This then often causes us to experience the six afflictions. We cling to an afflicted sense of self; we feel greed, aversion, and so forth; and many thoughts well up in our minds. We act and then experience the karmic result of that act. That causes us to experience the afflictions. This then causes us to act again and accumulate more karma. In this way we are caught in the cycle of interdependence that keeps spinning around and around. We experience feeling, which leads to craving. Craving leads to grasping, which leads to becoming, then birth, and finally aging and death. In this way, we cycle through the twelve links of interdependence, producing the appearances of this world.

We need a way to put a stop to this; we need an antidote. What is the antidote?

When that happens, it is important to possess the oral instructions on taking sickness as the path, taking joy and sorrow as the path, taking disturbing emotions as the path, and so forth.

The remedies are: first, taking sickness as the path; second, taking joy and sorrow as the path; third, taking afflictions or disturbing emotions as the path; and fourth, taking the bardo as the path, which is indicated by the phrase "and so forth" in the text. These four instructions are extremely important for us. When we get sick, for example, we do not want to just lie there enduring the pain and suffering of the illness. If we follow these instructions, when we get sick and maintain our practice, the illness will not be able to harm us, so the instructions on taking sickness as the path are important. Similarly, there are the instructions on taking joy and sorrow as the path. We sometimes feel joy or sorrow, which might lead us to experience one of the afflictions. But it is important that we do not lose control of ourselves to the afflictions. If we feel joy, we should not cling to the joy. If we feel pain, we should not react with aversion or be afraid of it. This is why we need the instructions on taking joy and sorrow as the path. When the disturbing emotions and other afflictions arise, we should not lose control of ourselves to them; we need to take them as the path. If we are overcome by the afflictions, we will accumulate karma, which will make us wander in samsara. This is why it is so important not to let ourselves be controlled by the afflictions. We need to use the experience and realization developed through our meditation to take all of these situations as the path.

We need to take everything as the path, but what does this really mean? How can we take all these situations as the path? Khenpo Gangshar says:

> But, if you simply rest in naturalness, the essence of all these applications, it will suffice.

Taking these situations as the path means to simply rest in the essence, naturalness. If you are sick, if you feel joy or sorrow, or if you experience one of the afflictions, simply rest within the natural unaltered essence of mind in the resting meditation of a kusulu. That is how we can take these situations as the path; that is all we need to do. This is the real essence of the instructions.

Resting in the natural state does not mean that you cannot think about things or work. The idea is to rest in the natural state and think at the same time. If you can do that, you can think things through and work, but there are no painful or sharp feelings. Sometimes strong afflictions such as anger and jealousy create obstacles for us, but when we take the afflictions as the path, they no longer have such power. We can rest in naturalness while continuing to work and fulfilling our responsibilities. There is a particular feeling that arises when we rest in naturalness; we must not forget that feeling and must always try to recall it.

14

TAKING JOY
AND SORROW AS
THE PATH

THE FIRST OF THE FOUR applications taught in these instructions is taking joy and sorrow as the path. We experience many different joys and sorrows. When we do, we have a lot of thoughts. This produces a lot of afflictions, and many feelings arise. So we need to make sure that joy and sorrow do not harm us. If fact, we can even use them as a way to develop our experience, realization, and samadhi meditation. If we can take joy and sorrow as the path, this life will be peaceful and happy.

Joy and sorrow are just thoughts—perhaps that makes them easiest to take as the path. Khenpo Gangshar says:

> If you feel happy when meeting with good conditions and
> sad when encountering negative circumstances and indulge
> in the feeling of happiness when happy and the feeling of
> sadness when sad, you will accumulate immense karma.

Normally, when we encounter good conditions, everything is going well, and other people respect and praise us, we feel good and joyful. We are happy. Sometimes we encounter bad circumstances—nothing goes well, things seem hard, and all we hear are unkind and hurtful words—and we feel unhappy about it. We might feel pain and discomfort. That is just how things are.

But what happens when we feel happy or unhappy? If we indulge in our feelings, we will perform many karmic actions. When we are happy about a good situation, we feel attachment to it. But often we are not satisfied with the situation. It does not live up to what we wanted and so we indulge in the feelings of happiness. We want more and more, and then our attachment grows stronger and stronger; we cling harder and harder.

When we indulge in our sadness, we think, "Oh, poor me!" It just gets worse and worse, and we get more and more depressed. Then we get upset and feel angry or jealous. Thus joy and excitement lead to more and more clinging; sorrow leads to anger and jealousy. As a result of either of these, we perform some sort of strong karmic act and accumulate more and more karma.

So what should we do? All we really need to do is relax. But how do we do that? When we experience joy or sorrow, what do we need to do?

> Therefore, you must immediately recognize a thought, be it
> happy or sad, in any circumstances, positive or negative.

Sometimes happy thoughts will arise in our minds, and sometimes unhappy thoughts arise. Whether the circumstances are positive or negative or the thoughts are happy or unhappy, we need to immediately recognize thoughts when they arise—"I just had a thought. I'm feeling happy. I'm feeling unhappy." In order to do that, we need to have mindfulness and awareness. When we get distracted, we don't recognize when thoughts of pleasure or displeasure arise. So we need to maintain our mindfulness. A thought arises, we recognize it, and we think, "That's a happy thought that I was following." Another thought arises and we think, "That's an unhappy thought that I was following." When we are feeling sad, we should not let ourselves be overcome by sadness. Instead, we should recognize and know that we are feeling sad. Similarly, if we are overcome by thoughts of joy, we get confused. That is not what we want. So when a thought of

joy arises, we need to recognize it immediately and know what it is.
First we have to know what is happening.

But what do we do once we have recognized a thought?

> After recognition, you should rest in naturalness. Look into
> the one who feels happy or sad, without repressing one feel-
> ing or encouraging the other. Your clear, empty, and naked
> mind-essence, free from any concern about joy or sorrow,
> freely becomes the innate state of awareness.

Normally we think to ourselves that we need to cling to the things
that we like. When we have unpleasant feelings toward something
we want to push it away and reject it. We feel that we can't let ourselves feel any suffering. But we should not do that. We should not
repress some thoughts or encourage others. Instead, we should just
rest naturally. There are many different ways, such as the techniques
taught in the foundation vehicle or viewing them as emptiness in the
mahayana, but in this tradition of resting in the nature of mind, the
method is to not block or repress any feelings. When we are unhappy,
we should not block it or look at it as some sort of a fault or problem.
In this way, we do not repress anything, nor do we indulge in anything, thinking it is good. Instead, we let the essence of what is feeling
joy and what is feeling sorrow settle naturally into the nature of the
mind. Look into the essence of the mind that feels that happiness.
Look at the essence of the mind that feels unhappiness. There is no
solid thing that is a feeling of happiness. There is no solid thing that
is a feeling of unhappiness. Then just rest easily within that awareness. Resting loose and relaxed within that awareness is what Khenpo
Gangshar means by the phrase "resting in naturalness."

In doing so, we take the experience we gain from the resting meditation of the kusulu and use it here to take joy and sorrow as the path.
When we do this, whatever happens, whether good or bad, joyful or
sad, we will not think to ourselves, "This is extraordinarily great!" and
feel attached to it, or "That's terrible," and get depressed and fearful.
Instead of getting involved in it, we will look at its essence. The essence of the mind is clear. The essence of that clarity is empty. The

essence of emptiness is naked. Then you can rest within this, loose and relaxed. If you feel happy, you are not overcome by happiness. If you are unhappy, you are not overcome by fear or suffering. We do not need to exchange the feelings or alter them in any way. Simply rest, seeing them as they are. This is taking joy and sorrow as the path.

15

TAKING PAIN
AND ILLNESS AS
THE PATH

I N OUR HUMAN LIVES, we get sick, and we need to be able to take that sickness as the path. When we are sick, we often feel uncomfortable in our bodies and unhappy in our minds. Our body is just something made of flesh, bones, and blood. When conditions are adverse or there are no favorable circumstances, our bodies will fall ill. We might get extremely sick and feel intolerable pain. What can we do in this situation? We need to develop the ability to take this sickness as the path.

Sickness and pain are feelings that take the form of suffering. When we do not have any instructions, sickness can be unbearable. We are overwhelmed by the sickness and oppressed by suffering. We need a method to make sure that the pain and illness cannot harm us, but that alone is not enough. We also need a way to make pain and illness a companion and helper in our practice. This is the practice of taking illness as the path.

Khenpo Gangshar says:

> Furthermore, when your body falls sick, don't indulge in the illness, but rest in naturalness. Look into the painful sensation itself. The pain doesn't cease when resting like that. However, you will directly realize the innate state of

awareness free from any thought about where it hurts, what hurts, how it hurts, as well as the subject and object of the pain. At that moment the sickness grows less intense and becomes somewhat insubstantial.

When you get sick, you should not indulge in the illness. Do not focus on the pain, thinking, "I'm sick. I have a headache. My tooth hurts." That is indulging in the sickness. Pain and sickness just happen, and when they do, we cannot just stop the sensation. Instead, we can rest, relaxing our mind and letting it settle in naturalness in relation to the essence of that sensation itself without any feeling of displeasure or not wanting it, looking at the essence of the sensation itself. In the sutras, this is called the foundation of mindfulness of feeling.

The pain does not necessarily stop, but when we look at the essence of the pain, its essence is empty; the pain is just an appearance that arises through interdependence. There is no thought of what hurts, how it hurts, where it hurts, what causes the pain, or who feels the pain. Although the pain does not immediately disappear, it does not have such a strong grip on us as it did before—it diminishes a bit and feels less solid or real. Does the pain stop? It does not—pain and sickness do occur because of the illusory body of flesh and blood. But in the naked state of awareness, it does not really harm us. Pain and sickness might not disappear, but in comparison to times when we did not have any experience of looking at the nature of our mind, they are weaker and do not hurt us as much as they did before. This is what we call taking pain and illness as the path.

When Khenpo Gangshar gave me these instructions, he went through each point in order. When he got to the instructions on taking sickness as the path, he pinched my cheek with his right hand. "Does that hurt?" he asked. "Don't have any thoughts about whether it is good or bad, just look at the essence of the pain." When I looked at the essence of the pain, it did not stop, but I did have the feeling it could not really do anything bad to me. It actually felt insubstantial, as it is described here, and I had the thought, "That's really how it is."

For beginners, taking a serious illness or strong pain as the path is a bit difficult, but this is a way that you can practice taking illness or pain as the path yourself: pinch the skin on your arm hard. At first it really hurts, but look directly at the essence of the pain and rest in meditation. Look at its essence and ask yourself, where is the pain? What is it like? What is its nature? As you look at it, the pain does not disappear, but it does not hurt as much as it did before. You can then use this as an exercise and then try to practice it when you actually do fall ill or experience pain, first with minor complaints and then gradually with stronger pain. That is taking pain and illness as the path. When Khenpo Gangshar taught this to me, I was really glad to learn that there were methods like this.

If you have a high level of realization, you can take sickness as the path; it will not really hurt you. For example, when the Sixteenth Karmapa fell ill with cancer, his doctor was a student of Trungpa Rinpoche named Mitchell Levy. When Dr. Levy was interviewed for the film *The Lion's Roar,* he was asked what the Karmapa's illness was like. He replied that such cancer usually creates almost unbearable pain and suffering, but the Gyalwang Karmapa did not seem to have that experience. When asked how he was doing, the Karmapa replied that he was fine and doing well. The reason this happened was because the Karmapa took his illness as the path. The illusory body of flesh and blood itself was sick, but the illness was not accompanied by much pain and the Karmapa was not particularly harmed by his illness. This is the sort of experience that can happen if we practice these instructions. We need to take illness as the path, but sometimes people think that if you practice Dharma you do not need to get medical treatment. This is not what it means to take illness as the path. Everything is interdependent; you must get medical treatment. It is not mentioned here, but in *Moonbeams of Mahamudra,* in the context of taking situations as the path, Takpo Tashi Namgyal says not to do anything stupid: you must get medical treatment.

When taking sickness as the path, we do not experience much suffering from the illness. We rest in samadhi without being overwhelmed by the pain. It becomes a favorable condition for our meditation. But this does not mean we should not get medical treatment.

16

TAKING AFFLICTIONS
AND EMOTIONS
AS THE PATH

WE ALSO NEED TO TAKE the afflictions as the path. This is very important because if we are unable to take them as the path, no matter how good our practice may be, we will be overcome by the afflictions. The afflictions are going to arise. They come out of the power of our imprints from the past. The main afflictions are greed, aversion, delusion, pride, and jealousy, which the Buddha described as the five poisons. When they occur, they create pain in our minds and suffering in our bodies. They lead us to do things that harm ourselves and others, which will bring us bad results. We lose control over ourselves to the afflictions, which necessarily creates many difficulties and suffering for ourselves and others. This is why these are called afflictions, and why they are said to have an aspect of suffering.

The Tibetan word *nyönmong* and the Sanskrit word *klesha* are often translated into English as "disturbing emotions" or "negative emotions." But when we translate it this way, sometimes people have too broad a conception of what they are—they think all emotions are afflictions. The Tibetan *nyönmong* does not include feelings such as love, compassion, devotion, regret, guilt, or sadness. These are strong feelings that are called emotions in English but are not nyönmong or afflictions. The afflictions include those things that naturally bring harm to ourselves and others, such as greed, aversion, delusion, pride, and envy, which are mentioned here. I think it is important to make this distinction.

Because we are ordinary individuals, the afflictions will naturally occur from time to time. No one can give us a medicine to stop them, nor can anyone else prevent them from happening. Actually, the afflictions themselves will naturally disappear when we practice. The reason is that they are just a type of thought. Like anything else in the mind, they appear to us, but if you look at their nature, you will not find anything solid about them, no matter how strong they may seem. In essence, they are just a thought in the mind.

Although the afflictions are just thoughts, if we lose control of ourselves to them, we will commit bad actions. As Shantideva says in *The Way of the Bodhisattva:*

> If all the gods and demigods besides
> Together came against me as my foes,
> They would be powerless to throw me down
> To fires of hell of Unrelenting Pain.
> And yet the mighty fiend of my afflictions
> Flings me in an instant headlong down
> To where the mighty lord of mountains
> Would be burned, its very ashes all consumed.

At some point, someone will do something bad to us, causing us some sort of pain or suffering. But can that person, that enemy, cast us down into the deepest of the hells, the Hell of Unrelenting Pain, and make us experience the horrendous suffering there? They cannot. But when our enemies the afflictions harm us, they can throw us right down into the Hell of Unrelenting Pain. This is how powerful they are.

Yet the essence of the afflictions is naturally empty. As it says in *The Way of the Bodhisattva:*

> Miserable defilements, scattered by the eye of wisdom!

When we look at them carefully, with intelligence, they do not have any essence. When a strong affliction such as anger arises, we have the unbearable feeling that we need to hurt someone or say something mean, but where is the affliction? What is its essence? When we examine it and meditate, we see that its essence is naturally empty. If we realize this, it naturally has no power and disappears. This is why many instruction manuals say that when the afflictions arise, we should not block them or reject them. Do not follow them either, but instead look at their essence. If we do that, when greed, anger, or delusion arise, they will naturally dissipate and become nothing. This is how you should take them as the path.

IDENTIFYING THE AFFLICTIONS AND THEIR RESULTS

Khenpo Gangshar writes:

> A person who has one disturbing emotion will also possess the others. But due to the differences in people, some will have more anger, some more stinginess, some more dullness, some more desire, some more envy, and some will have a greater portion of pride. That is why there are different types of buddha families.

A person who has any one of the afflictions or disturbing emotions will also have all of the others—someone who has greed will also have anger and all the other afflictions. They may or may not be manifest, but they are present until such time as they have been completely abandoned. But because people are all different, some have more anger. Some are stingier. Some are more deluded, some greedier, more envious, or more prideful. These differences come about because of the imprints to which we have been habituated throughout beginningless time.

There are different types of people, and because of this, there are also different buddha families. Those who have more anger are in the family of the Buddha's body of Akshobhya. Pride and stinginess both correspond to the family of the Buddha's qualities, the family of Ratnasambhava. Those who are most afflicted by desire belong to the family of speech. The envious belong to the family of activity, and the deluded belong to the family of the Buddha's mind. These are the families that are pointed out to us during vajrayana empowerments when we cast a stick into the mandala to see what family it points to.

But what are the afflictions? We need to be able to identify each of the different afflictions—anger, stinginess, delusion, desire, envy, and pride—and learn to recognize them. Khenpo Gangshar describes the characteristics of each of them in order.

The first is anger:

> The disturbing emotion of anger is an agitated state of mind caused by a painful sensation based on an unpleasant object.

Anger arises when we encounter an object that is unpleasant. We see something unpleasant that does not fit with our wishes. We do not like it and get annoyed. Perhaps someone said something nasty, someone hurt us, or we are experiencing some sort of difficulty or unpleasant situation. The object that provokes our displeasure might be another sentient being, or it might be an inanimate object like a rock. Sometimes we encounter unpleasant people and sometimes we encounter unpleasant things. As a result of either of these circumstances, we experience displeasure in our mind. That stirs up our mind, and then we start to struggle and fight. This happens most often with regard to other sentient beings, although we do sometimes struggle and fight against material objects as well. That is aversion, or anger.

Sometimes we encounter sentient beings or material objects that are very pleasant, and we feel stingy.

> Stinginess is the inability to give away to others some attractive object because of retaining a tight clinging to owning it.

When we have something, we think it is our own. We cling to it tightly and feel like we could not possibly give it away or lend it to anyone. If we were to see other people using or enjoying that object, we would feel upset. That is stinginess.

The third affliction is delusion, or dullness:

> Dullness is like darkness and is the root of all evil. It is the
> lack of recognizing one's essence and it obscures the nature
> of things.

Delusion is simply not knowing or not understanding. When Khenpo
Gangshar says that "it is the lack of recognizing one's essence," this
means that we don't clearly see what it is. Because we do not recognize the nature of our minds, we do not really understand how things
are; it prevents us from seeing the nature of things. Through not
knowing this nature, our delusion gets stronger and then we become
more envious, angry, or greedy. The afflictions gradually develop and
then all kinds of faults and problems can arise. In and of itself, this
dullness is not particularly strong and is not such a great fault, but
because it causes all the other afflictions to develop, it is the root of
all our faults, problems, and difficulties.

When we talk about other afflictions such as hatred, greed, jealousy, stinginess, and so forth, they are easy to identify. But delusion is
naturally unclear and foggy. Since its nature is simply not knowing,
it is hard to say, "This is delusion." This makes it difficult to recognize.
It is darkness or blankness: our failure to see the nature of our minds
obscures the nature of things so that we do not know it either. It is
the root of all faults.

Delusion is just ignorance and dullness. With anger you can say,
"I got angry" or "Now my anger has gone away." But we never think,
"My ignorance has gone away." We are always deluded and ignorant.
Delusion is continually present until we abandon it through medita-
tion. As we study and practice and the essence of delusion gets clearer
and clearer, the fogginess of delusion gradually lessens.

The fourth affliction is desire, or greed:

> Desire is to accept, long for, and feel attached to pleasant
> things like sights or sounds and so forth. In particular, car-
> nal lust for the union of male and female is the primary
> attachment.

The objects we perceive—forms we see with our eyes, sounds we hear
with our ears, scents we smell with our nose, tastes we taste with

our tongue, and the sensations that we feel with our body—can be either pleasant or unpleasant. When they are pleasant, we want to cling to them and get more of them. We think, "I want that! That's really great." We want them and feel attached to them. That is what we mean by greed or desire in general, but among all the types of desire, the root is sexual desire. Thus desire means wanting and being attached to pleasurable things.

The fifth affliction is envy:

> Envy is to reject and therefore disapprove of the virtues of someone who is higher than or equal to oneself.

Sometimes we see people who are superior or equal to ourselves and feel envious of them. We generally feel envious of those better than us or our equals; we do not feel envious of our inferiors. Perhaps someone has more qualities or education, and we do not like it; we cannot accept it. Sometimes we see someone who is on the same level as us, but we begin to suspect that they might end up better off than we are and cannot accept that, either. We see their qualities but cannot accept that they are qualities—we view them as faults. This is what we mean by envy.

The sixth of the afflictions is pride:

> Pride is to regard others as lower and to feel superior in either religious or mundane matters.

Pride primarily occurs when we regard other people to be lower than ourselves. There are two sorts of things we can feel pride about: religious matters and worldly matters. You might think you are a better Dharma practitioner than someone else or that you know more about the Dharma. Or you might consider yourself superior in terms of your work or some other worldly quality. In either case, thinking "I'm better than them" or "I'm the best" is what we mean by pride.

Most of the time, pride arises when we look at those we view as inferior. But if we look at it in more detail, there are seven types of pride: When we look at inferiors and perceive them as lower than us, that is called either just "pride" or "lesser pride." Sometimes we look at our equals and we think we are better than they are. That is called "superior pride." Sometimes we see someone who is our superior and we think, "I am that person's equal" or "I am better than that person." This is called "more proud than pride." When we see our body and minds and feel conceited, thinking "That is me," this is "pride in thinking *me*." When we think we have clairvoyance and other powers although we actually do not, this is the "pride of exaggeration." Sometimes we look at people who are superior to ourselves and think we are almost as good as they are. This is "pride in thinking *almost*." Sometimes we look at ourselves and perceive our own thoughts as qualities rather than faults. We think they are great. This is what we call "mistaken pride."

It is important for us to deal with our afflictions and not fall under their control, since these six different afflictions are each a cause for rebirth in one of the six realms of samsara. Khenpo Gangshar uses the first one, anger, as an example:

> These six disturbing emotions create the causes for the existence of the six classes of beings, such as rebirth in the hells through predominant anger.

When our predominant affliction is anger—when we have strong anger—this leads to rebirth in the hell realms. Similarly, strong stinginess leads to rebirth as a hungry ghost. Strong delusion or dullness leads to rebirth in the animal realm, strong desire to rebirth in the human realm, strong jealousy to rebirth as a demigod, and strong pride leads to rebirth in the realms of the gods of the desire realm. We will be reborn in the realm of samsara that corresponds to our strongest affliction.

NATURALLY LIBERATING THE AFFLICTIONS

What should we do when afflictions arise? How do we keep from falling under their control? The way to practice is to build upon the experience we have in the resting meditation of the kusulu: we can take them as the path within this meditation. As the instructions say:

Whenever one of them arises you must recognize it immediately. When recognizing it, don't reject it, don't accept it,
just rest in naturalness [looking] into that particular disturbing emotion. At that same moment it is self-liberated
and is called mirror-like wisdom, etc.

We are just ordinary beings, so the afflictions do arise in us. Normally
we do not recognize when or how the afflictions arise and so we lose
control of ourselves to them. What we need to do instead is recognize
them immediately when they occur. If it was anger, we need to be
able to say, "This is anger." If we do not sense that we have become
angry, we will be overcome by the anger; we will feel badly, get into
fights, or say something hurtful. This happens because we did not
recognize the anger. So we need to recognize the anger immediately
when it arises. It is the same with stinginess, desire, pride, or jealousy:
we need to recognize them as soon as they occur. Sometimes they
well up naturally and it is difficult to see them, but we need to recognize them.

Once we have recognized an affliction, what do we need to do?
We do not need to tell ourselves how bad it is and try to stop it. We
should not think, "I should not let myself get angry. I should not
let myself feel envious. I should not feel that." We do not need to
do anything to repress it. At the same time, we should not be like
ordinary people and take the affliction up, follow it, and indulge in
it. We should not think it is good and that we need to accomplish
something with it. If we do not recognize the affliction when it occurs and end up following it, it will get stronger and stronger and
then lead to even more afflictions. If we get angry and then we follow the anger, we will act it out with our body and speech. If we
follow pride or jealousy, they will just get stronger and stronger. That
is why we do not follow our afflictions. We need to avoid both of
these approaches.

So what should we do? Whenever an affliction occurs, we should
just look at it and rest in naturalness. When the affliction of anger
occurs, we should look at its essence and ask, "Where did the anger
arise?" Anger seems like something strong from the outside, but if

we actually look at its nature, where did it come from? What is its essence? When we investigate this, we see that its essence is empty. If we then rest in the expanse of the affliction itself, it naturally disappears. Whether it is anger, desire, or delusion, when we rest in the expanse of the natural state, it is liberated the moment it appears. Many great masters in the past have explained this with the example of tying a snake in a knot. When you tie a snake in a knot, the snake will gradually loosen the knot and untie itself. It is the same here: the afflictions are self-liberated and naturally disappear when we look at them and see their essence.

If we do not look at the essence of the afflictions, they will grow stronger and stronger, and we will end up committing many harmful acts. So we need to apply a remedy for the afflictions. The remedy is not to reject, block, or suppress the emotion—as scientists these days say, repressing your disturbing emotions will lead to illness in your body. We Buddhists also say that you should not block your emotions. This, however, does not mean that we should just follow our afflictions and go wherever they lead us. Instead, we need to look at the essence of the afflictions, and then they will be self-liberated. This means that they will just naturally be pacified, and become the root that will be transformed into wisdom in the future, such as with the transformation of aversion into mirror-like wisdom.

These instructions are also given in a song by Ratna Lingpa, who was one of the great tertöns, or treasure discoverers, who have revealed many of Guru Rinpoche's teachings. There have been many tertöns over the centuries, but the main ones are the twenty-five Lingpas, of whom five are considered to be like kings. These five are Sangye Lingpa, who lived in the central region; Dorje Lingpa, in the east; Ratna Lingpa, in the south; Pema Lingpa, in the west; and Karma Lingpa, in the north. They found many profound and helpful Dharma teachings. For example, The Tibetan Book of the Dead is a treasure of Karma Lingpa that advises us on how to protect ourselves in the bardo after death, instructing us on the practices of the peaceful and wrathful deities. Ratna Lingpa, whom Khenpo Gangshar quotes, was one of these five king-like Lingpas.

Ratna Lingpa gave many of his teachings in the form of songs, and these songs were compiled in three different treasuries. This song is taken from his *Second Treasury*. It teaches how to take anger, delusion, pride, and desire as the path, and it gives essentially the same instruction as Khenpo Gangshar gave above. The first verse teaches how to deal with anger:

> The essence of your angry mind is clear awareness,
> Bright and empty the moment you recognize it.
> This nature is called mirror-like wisdom.
> Young maid, let's rest in the natural state.

Anger does sometimes arise, and when it does, it is very clear—our awareness is sharp and clear at that time. If our attention is directed outside ourselves at the object we are angry at, we will not recognize the essence of our anger. Because we do not know its essence, it grows stronger and stronger. We are afflicted by one disturbing emotion, and that leads to more afflictions, which cause us to perform harmful acts and accumulate bad karma. For that reason, we should not follow our anger. Instead, we need to turn our attention inward and look at the essence of the anger. When we recognize that we have gotten angry, we need to look at the essence of anger: where is the anger? When we look at its nature, we cannot find it; it cannot be established as anything. We see that it does not truly exist. It is empty. But at the same time it does not stop: it is clear—bright and empty the moment we recognize it. This is the same as in Khenpo Gangshar's instructions.

The anger does not become bright and empty the moment we recognize it. When Ratna Lingpa says "the moment you recognize it," that means that it has been like that all the time, but it is only now that we see it. When you get angry, look at the essence of the anger itself, and see that there is nothing to the essence of the anger and that it is the union of clarity and emptiness. The anger becomes natural, and among the five wisdoms it becomes mirror-like wisdom. In the last line, "Young maid, let's rest in the natural state," Ratna Lingpa addresses his wife, to whom he says that he practices within this state. This teaches how to take anger as the path.

The second of the afflictions that he discusses is delusion.

> The essence of your dull mind is clear self-awareness,
> Wide open the moment you look into your natural face.
> This vital nature is called dharmadhatu wisdom.
> Young maid, let's rest in the natural state.

As we discussed above, delusion is foggy by nature. Delusion might be foggy and dull, but the nature of mind itself is always clear. It is always knowing; it can always understand something. When we experience delusion, we do not really see this, but actually the clarity of the mind never ceases. The mind is always clear and knowing; it never turns into something like a rock. The clear self-awareness is continually present and knowing. If we look into our natural face—if we look at the essence of the delusion itself—it is wide awake, which means that it is clear. It's like there is a little gap. This nature is called the dharmadhatu wisdom. When you look at the essence you see that it is clear and knowing, but also that it is empty.

Whenever any of the afflictions occurs, if you recognize it and look at its nature, you see that it does not have any real essence. It no longer takes the form of an affliction that is directed outward: it is looking inward at the essence of the dharma nature. For this reason, when we look at the essence of the affliction of delusion, it becomes dharmadhatu wisdom. The dharmadhatu is the aspect of emptiness. When you look at the essence of delusion, it naturally disappears into emptiness and becomes the essence of dharmadhatu wisdom. When he says, "Young maid, let's rest in the natural state," he means that this is how he takes delusion as the path, and that all his students should do this as well.

The third stanza discusses pride:

> The essence of your proud mind is the unfolding of self-
> awareness,
> Naturally empty the moment you rest, looking into your
> natural face.
> This state is called the wisdom of equality.
> Young maid, let's rest in the natural state.

Sometimes we think we are great—we think, "I'm something special!" However, when you look at the essence of pride, you cannot establish it as anything at all. It becomes nothing and empty of itself. Looking at this essence is called the wisdom of equality. When we think, "I'm great! I'm better than other people," we do not see the fundamental equality of ourselves and all other sentient beings. But when we look at the essence of pride to see where it is and what it is like, it naturally dissolves. When our pride has been quelled, we understand that all beings are essentially equal in the natural state. This isn't a conceptual thought that everyone is like ourselves; when pride is stilled, it naturally subsides into the essence of the wisdom of equality.

The last verse discusses the affliction of desire:

> The essence of your lustful mind is attachment for sure,
> The state of empty bliss, the moment you sustain it
>   without clinging.
> This nature is called discriminating wisdom.
> Young maid, let's rest in the natural state.

Whether you call it lust, desire, or greed, the desirous mind is basically craving—really wanting something and being attached to it. But when you do not follow it and are not attached to it, when you look into its essence, it is comfortable and blissful, and its essence is naturally empty. This is called discriminating wisdom. This means that you can look at everything and see it clearly; you know what everything is.

These four stanzas cover four of the afflictions, but there are still two that Khenpo Gangshar taught above but are not mentioned here: stinginess and jealousy. These two, however, can be considered to be subsumed under the four taught here: stinginess is included within desire, and envy is included within anger. Other afflictions, such as bearing grudges, spite, or hypocrisy, can also be considered part of these four. In this way, Ratna Lingpa's song tells us how to take all of the various afflictions as the path.

We must remember that we are all ordinary individuals, and as ordinary individuals we will sometimes experience the afflictions.

They are going to arise. But when they do arise, it is not necessarily bad. The afflictions naturally arise because of our imprints from beginningless time in samsara. If they aren't bad, does that mean that we should just follow them? It does not mean that. If we follow them, it will create a lot of problems. What we really need to do is know the essence of the affliction. We need to look at the essence of the affliction, and if we do this, we will see that it cannot be established as anything in itself. This is a characteristic of the afflictions. Even though afflictions do not truly exist, they occur. When the afflictions arise, they seem extremely strong and solid. That is how they appear, but that does not mean that we need to either repress them or indulge in them. We just need to know them as they are. They are like bubbles in water—the center of a bubble is empty, so it will naturally disappear. When you look at the afflictions and see that their nature is naturally empty, they just disappear on their own.

METHODS FOR DEALING WITH THE AFFLICTIONS

Following this is a discussion of the different ways we can deal with the afflictions. In general, there are three different ways we can use the afflictions: to reject and block them, to view them as empty, or to follow them:

> But if you regard disturbing emotions as faults and reject them, they may be temporarily suppressed but not cut from their root. Consequently, at some point, the poisonous remnant will reemerge, as is the case of the mundane dhyana states.

When any of the afflictions occur, from one perspective it is good to realize that that they are problems, but that does not mean that they should be blocked or repressed. If we just think that the afflictions are no good and that we must not let them arise, we might succeed in suppressing them and stop them for some period of time, but we will not be able to uproot them entirely. Since they have not been eradicated, for a while it may seem as if there are no afflictions, but they will inevitably resurface. This is like the mundane dhyana meditations that some non-Buddhists practice, particularly in India. These are very deep states of samadhi during which the afflictions are suppressed and do not manifest for some period of time. But the afflictions have not been uprooted entirely. Eventually the meditation will wear off, the latent afflictions will reappear, and the practitioner will continue to wander in samsara. This is not what we need to do.

Another approach would be to just see all the disturbing emotions as emptiness:

> On the one hand, when you regard disturbing emotions as emptiness, your practice turns into "taking emptiness as the path" and not the disturbing emotions. Thus your practice doesn't become the short path, the special quality of mantra.

There are two different paths we can follow: taking emptiness as the path and taking the afflictions as the path. When we think that the afflictions are emptiness and meditate on that, this is not taking the afflictions as the path, it is taking emptiness as the path. We do not normally think that things are empty, but if we consider that they are empty and meditate on that, we can gradually progress down the path. This is not the short path; it is a long and difficult path. It requires developing certainty that phenomena are empty, meditating on emptiness, and then gradually gaining an experience of emptiness, so it does not have the special quality of the vajrayana. Can we give up the afflictions through this path? We can, but it is not a path whereby we can give them up quickly.

The next thing we could do is indulge in the afflictions by following them.

> On the other hand, if you indulge in the disturbing emotions, thinking they are something concrete, it is like eating a poisonous plant and is the cause that binds you to samsara, just like the copulation of ordinary people.

If we don't take control over the afflictions and instead fall under their control, it is like eating poison. For instance, if you eat a poisonous

plant you will get sick, die, or experience all sorts of different sufferings. Likewise, if we think that the afflictions are real and true, so
we should follow them, this binds us to samsara. It is not the cause of
freedom from samsara; it just increases and intensifies the afflictions.
"The copulation of ordinary people" should be understood as acting
out of the power of lust. This is why acting upon the afflictions is not
appropriate.

These three ways of dealing with the afflictions—suppressing
them, viewing them as emptiness, and indulging them—will not
work. What we need to do instead is take them as the path. But how
can we put that into practice? Here Khenpo Gangshar gives us an
analogy:

> For these reasons, just as poison can be extracted from a poi-
> sonous plant and taken as a medicine, the special quality of
> this teaching lies in the fact that any disturbing emotion
> that may arise is wisdom the moment you relax in natural-
> ness. Look directly into it, don't deliberately reject it, regard
> it as a fault, indulge in it concretely, or regard it as a virtue.

There are many plants that will harm you if you eat them as they are,
but if you extract the poison from the plant, the poison itself can be
transformed into medicine. This is a common way to make medicines. We need the poison, but we can't take it directly—we have to
convert it into medicine. We need to work with our afflictions in the
same way: when an affliction arises, should we think that it is bad
and needs to be blocked? We must not block or repress it at all. Nor
should we, thinking that they are good and wonderful qualities, follow our afflictions. For example, if you get angry, do not think, "I'm a
great hero. I can go out and fight!" Do not fall into either extreme: do
not see the affliction as a quality and take it up; do not see it as a fault
and try to repress it. Afflictions are going to arise, and when they do,
we need to identify them immediately. We need to look directly into
the essence of the affliction the moment it arises and relax into naturalness within the recognition of the nature of the affliction. When
you see the essence of the affliction, it becomes the union of clarity
and emptiness, and at that point it is transformed into wisdom. The

affliction is immediately quelled and becomes mirror-like wisdom, the wisdom of equality, discriminating wisdom, or dharmadhatu wisdom, as described above. This is the special quality of this teaching. Whichever affliction occurs, if you want to take it as the path, just look directly at its nature and it will naturally be pacified.

Khenpo Gangshar also briefly discusses other instructions on taking afflictions as the path:

> Beyond this, if you are interested in the system of direct instructions, such as the teachings on the path of means, you must learn them in detail from the oral instructions of your master.

There are many practices of the path of means, such as the creation stage, tummo, the illusory body, and many others, but these need direct instructions which tell you specifically what to do and how—how to visualize, etc. If you want to practice, you need to request and receive the instructions from a lama and then practice them. But what Khenpo Gangshar is teaching here is a general method for dealing with the afflictions.

APPLYING THIS METHOD TO OTHER EMOTIONS

These instructions on taking the afflictions as the path teach us how to deal with the six afflictions of anger, stinginess, delusion, desire, jealousy, and pride, but there are also other emotions we can feel. Sometimes we get depressed or discouraged. Sometimes we feel regret and guilt, and sometimes we are afraid, or even terrified. The Buddha taught that these are not afflictions—they are emotions and they may be disturbing, but they are not afflictions. These emotions arise and they can create discomfort or difficulty, but they do not generally directly lead us to harm other people. They are not causes for future pain and unhappiness. For example, when we feel regret and guilt, we feel unhappy, but it does not generally motivate us to do something hurtful. That is why such emotions are not included among the afflictions. However, they are unpleasant and even painful experiences, so we need a way to help ourselves when they arise. The way to deal with any depression, anxiety, or fear is to look at the nature of the emotion and rest in the natural state. When you look at the essence of fear, the fear disappears without harming you. When you feel depressed, look at the essence of the depression, and it will dissipate. You can do the same thing with regret and guilt: when you look at the essence of guilt and see that its essence cannot be established as anything, there is no way it can hurt you. We can use the same instructions for taking the afflictions as the path with the emotions of fear, regret, guilt, and depression as well.

17

TAKING THE BARDO
AS THE PATH

DEATH IS SOMETHING THAT is going to happen to all of us. We will die and experience the bardo state. There is no way to avoid it. Since it is one hundred percent certain that we will experience this, we need instructions that can help. There are many instructions in Buddhism on what we should do in the bardo, especially in the secret mantra vajrayana, but among all of them, Khenpo Gangshar's are among the simplest and easiest. Yet they are also extremely beneficial and powerful.

What is death? During this life we have both a body and a mind, and these two are connected. Our body is a composite, a material aggregate of all our flesh, blood, and bones, but our mind is clear awareness. During this life, they coexist: the mind thinks of the body as its own. It resides within the body, supported by the body. But at some point, the body and mind will separate. It is like a person inside a house: while inside, the person is supported by the house, but eventually one goes outside. Similarly, our internal mind resides within the external body, but the mind must leave the body at some point. That point when the mind and body separate is what we call death.

When the body and the mind separate, they part from each other, but that does not mean that the mind stops. The clear part of the mind is unceasing and continues as it had been before. The clarity continues at the time of death without changing. The consciousness in the bardo is not born anew; it is a continuation of the stream of consciousness from the previous life.

During this life there are the appearances of this life, but when we die, these appearances will dissolve and the appearances of our next rebirth will eventually begin. The period between these two is what we call the bardo or in-between state. For example, when you flip from one television channel to another, it seems as if you go straight from one channel to the next, but what really happens is that when you are watching channel one, decide you do not like it, and flip the channel, the picture on the screen collapses into itself and ceases momentarily before the image on the next channel appears. When you decide you do not like that channel either and change the channel again, that picture collapses and then another appears. Every time you change the channel, the old image collapses before the new one appears. In between channels is a short, empty pause. That is what we would call the bardo if we were talking about the appearances of our lives.

TV channels are not important, but the bardo is. The point when the appearances of this life stop and we exchange them for the appearance of a new life is critical. The reason is because if we are not overcome by fear or the afflictions and can maintain a good, calm, and gentle state of mind, it will help us to make the appearances of the next life positive. If instead we are overpowered by fear and afflictions during the bardo and our mind is agitated by difficult feelings and afflictions such as anger, our next life will be tumultuous—we will not be able to take a good rebirth. In order to prevent that, we must be able to control ourselves during the bardo. The way to make sure that we will be able to do that is to think about the bardo beforehand. If we contemplate and prepare for it now, our minds will be loose and relaxed when we arrive at the time of death and during the bardo as well. We should not think that there is no need to worry and put it aside. If you do that, when you suddenly find yourself in the bardo, you will feel afraid, depressed, or even angry, which will lead to many difficulties. That is why it is important to practice taking the bardo as the path now.

The reason we experienced the confused perceptions of this life is that the life wind is currently within the central channel. When the life wind loses its strength, the white drop we received from our father and the red drop we received from our mother will come together and meet in our heart. Once they meet, the appearances of the bardo will occur. At the time of death, all the imprints of confused appearance collapse into the nature of the mind and the dharma nature. If someone has a good, strong meditation practice, this moment is very beneficial because the path luminosity one learns to recognize in meditation practice and the ground luminosity of the dharma nature come together like the reunion of a mother and child. If we can rest in samadhi within this union, it will be very beneficial. But if we do not have such a strong meditation practice, we will not recognize the ground luminosity, and it will be as if we just fell unconscious. We will not have the feeling that appearances of the dharma nature and the nature of mind are occurring. When we arise from that, the body and mind will have separated.

The mind is made up of eight different consciousnesses. In each of these consciousnesses, there are fifty-one different mental factors that can occur, which are like the coarse thoughts that we have. The bare consciousnesses themselves normally reside within our heart. When the mind and body separate at death, the eight consciousnesses are released from the body and appear as the forty-two peaceful deities including the eight great male bodhisattvas, the eight great female bodhisattvas, and others. The motion of the coarse thoughts—the fifty-one mental factors—normally occurs within the brain, but when released from the body at death, the fifty-one factors appear as the fifty-one bloodthirsty, wrathful deities. If we have done creation-stage visualization practices, we can recognize these deities, which will allow us to take a good rebirth. However, if our practice is not stable, we will not recognize the deities, and we will be overcome by the afflictions of desire and aversion, or by sheer terror. Then all the confused perceptions of the bardo will occur. This is why it is so important to do practices to prepare for the bardo, as described in various instruction manuals and teachings.

Familiarizing Yourself with Natural Luminosity and Resonance

Khenpo Gangshar's instructions for taking the bardo as the path are simple, uncomplicated instructions that we can easily follow. To practice them, cover your eyes lightly or block your ears. There will be lights and sounds that naturally manifest. When you perceive these, rest naturally for a while. Khenpo Gangshar says:

> When you press your fingers on your ears or on your eyes, sounds naturally resound and colors and lights naturally manifest. Rest naturally for a long time and grow accustomed to the appearance of utterly empty forms that don't exist anywhere—neither outside, inside, nor in between. Since, at the time of death, there is nothing other than this, you will recognize these sounds, colors, and lights as your self-display and be liberated, just like meeting a person you already know or a child leaping onto its mother's lap.

His instructions are to close your eyes firmly so that external forms no longer appear. At first you only see blackness, but if you let your mind rest loose and relaxed within that blackness, gradually various lights will appear. There will be red, yellow, green, or blue lights—lights of many colors and shapes. As you keep looking, the lights will grow stronger and brighter. They are not necessarily any particular color or any particular shape. These appearances are what in the bardo we call the natural radiance of the dharma nature. When the eye faculty has stopped at death, the natural radiance of the dharma nature will occur, and if we have no experience of this, then we will wonder what these lights are. We will be terrified of these confused appearances. This is why we practice now: we look at the shapes and colors that appear when we close our eyes tightly. These lights appear, but there is nothing about them that can be established as real. Just rest loosely and naturally, looking at this without thinking of anything. When you do this, the empty lights of the dharma nature do not disappear, but your fear of them will diminish. This is how we take the natural radiance of the empty dharma nature as the path.

We can do something similar with our hearing. When resting in natural samadhi, clench your jaws together tightly and listen to what you hear. At first there isn't any sound, but then we begin to hear a slight roar in the background. As we rest loose and relaxed, the roaring will grow louder and louder until it is loud and clear. This sound is the natural sound of the empty dharma nature. This is not like the sound of playing gongs or drums—it is not any kind of external sound from some object. This sound has no real source or place that it comes from; it is the natural resonance of the dharma nature. As we listen to it, it grows stronger and stronger until it sounds like a thousand simultaneous thunderclaps.

This sound will also occur when we are in the bardo, and it is quite possible that we will be terrified of it when we hear it then. So we need listen to it now, so that it will not be so frightening when we hear it in the bardo. When we hear the natural resonance of the dharma nature, it does not have any source or any physical, material aspect; it is just empty, natural resonance. When we just listen to it, our minds relaxed and not altering anything, the sound does not disappear, but there is no object to be afraid of nor any way the sound can harm you. The sound no longer seems so oppressive in your ears.

Although Khenpo Gangshar's instructions say to press your eyes with your fingers, many physicians say that if you press your eyes in this way, it is possible to damage your vision, and if you block your ears you might damage your hearing. It is important not to injure yourself, but that does not mean you cannot do this practice—you do not necessarily have to take your hands and press your eyeballs and block your ears. Instead you can clench your jaws hard and close your eyes tight without pressing on them with your fingers, and these lights and sounds will appear anyway. You don't necessarily have to use your hands. For this reason, you should do this practice, but you must not plug your eyes and ears with your fingers. Just clench your teeth and close your eyes tight, and the lights and sounds will appear.

When I received these instructions from Khenpo Gangshar, he placed his two thumbs over my eyes and pressed lightly. He plugged my ear holes closed with his middle fingers. He asked me what I saw, but at first it was just blackness and I could not see or hear anything at all. However, as I let my mind relax and looked to see what appeared to my eyes and listened to the sounds coming through my ears, I gradually began to see various lights appear. They were various colors and shapes—some reddish, some greenish, some bluish. When I relaxed and listened, there was a roaring, thundering sound.

These lights and sounds are the natural appearance and resonance of the dharma nature. When your eyes are closed and your ears blocked, you are not looking at or listening to any external object. These are just the sounds and lights that naturally happen. When they appear, what you should do is rest naturally, looking at their nature. When you rest loosely, looking at the nature of the lights or the sounds, you see that the lights and sounds are naturally empty. When you see that, they are less overwhelming and terrible.

These lights and sounds are not outside of ourselves, nor are they inside, nor between the outside and inside. We cannot find any origin from which they arise. When we view them in this way, they dissolve into emptiness and any fear we may have experienced at first will disappear. We should meditate on these for a long time in order to grow accustomed to them.

The reason we need to getting used to these appearances is that, as it says here, the appearances we see at the time of death are no different from these. These lights and sounds will occur. The reason is that the eye and ear faculties have ceased functioning at that point. It seems pitch black at first, but gradually appearances will arise—the natural lights and sounds of the dharma nature will appear. If you have practiced and grown accustomed to them, you can rest within them and become liberated—they will not harm you. If you are not used to them and feel like you have never seen them before, then you might feel a bit afraid, wondering what they are. You will be frightened by the lights and sounds that naturally come from the dharma nature.

But if you recognize these appearances, as Khenpo Gangshar says, it will be like seeing an old acquaintance or a child leaping into his mother's lap. You will remember that this is just a natural appearance, that the natural empty sounds and sights of the dharma nature are going to happen and that there is no need to fear them. If you can think in this way and rest in meditation within the dharma nature, the lights will not overpower you and the sounds will not harm you in any way.

The instructions continue:

> This teaching corresponds to the key point of darkness instruction among the daylight instructions and darkness instructions for practicing the manifest aspect of the thögal of spontaneous presence. There are also the systems of practice based on the rising and setting rays at daytime and on the moonlight, electric light and lamps at nighttime.

These instructions are the same as the darkness instructions from the dzogchen tradition. There are two types of dzogchen practice: trekchö, or cutting through, and thögal, or the sudden leap. The primordially pure trekchö practices involve meditating on emptiness and the nature of mind itself. The thögal practices include meditating while looking at sunlight or an electric light in order to see the appearance of rainbows and drops, which are the daylight instructions. There are also practices of darkness instructions where one goes into a cave or another pitch-black place and meditates in utter darkness. These instructions are essentially the same as the darkness practices or a dark retreat. When doing those practices, one sees various lights and looks at their essence. The only distinction between these instructions and the darkness instructions is how elaborate the instructions are. The six applications of the Kalachakra practice also include daylight and darkness practices, and therefore this practice is similar to them, too. One can also do practices that involve looking at lights, moonlight, or various different types of lamps. If you want to do any of these types of practices then you should get instruction from a lama and meditate following their instructions. If you just do it on your own without any instructions, it will not be easy and you will have many difficulties and problems. This is why you should follow the instructions of a master.

In contrast to these other practices, Khenpo Gangshar's instructions are concise and easy to follow. He tells us how we should look at the lights and sounds that appear, but the way to take them as the path is the same as the same as before: just rest relaxed within them, not altering them in any way.

TAKING SLEEP AS THE PATH

Following this come the instructions on taking sleep as the path, which are an aid to taking the bardo as the path. There are many different practices and instructions for dreams. Generally, during the daytime we think about many different things, and then when we go to sleep at night, we recognize our dreams. Some of the practices then involve doing things like transforming your dreams—taking a bad dream and making it into a good dream, or emanating bodies in your dreams. There are these and other instructions on dream yogas, but Khenpo Gangshar's instructions on taking sleep as the path do not involve such mental effort. What are his instructions?

> Without depending on mental effort, such as emanations or transformations during the dream state, sleep in a state of undistracted naturalness. During that time, you may slip into deep sleep devoid of dreams. As soon as you awake you are vividly clear in the natural state. This is called the *luminosity of deep sleep.*

When you are first going to sleep, rest in equipoise through your mindfulness and awareness, and fall asleep within this state. Just sleep in the state of awareness, resting naturally within it. If you can sleep in this way without being distracted, your awareness is very clear and crisp. Sometimes you may sleep very deeply without many dreams and with no distraction. Then when you wake up, your mind is vividly clear and sharp within your previous practice and meditation. Things occur in your mind, but they do not distract you. You are loose and relaxed; there is no disturbance or turbulence during your sleep. This is called the luminosity of deep sleep because there are imprints of your samadhi.

Sometimes you might not sleep at all and instead remain very alert:

It may happen that sleep doesn't occur at all. Instead, you remain awake and vividly clear or you fall asleep. But, though various dreams take place, they are forgotten the moment you wake up the next morning with nothing to remember. That is the beginning of having purified dreams.

Sometimes you maintain your practice when you go to bed, but sleep does not come and you rest vividly, clearly, in meditation. Or if you do sleep, you might have some dreams, but they do not distract you. They do not seem solid or real. This is a sign that they are beginning to be purified.

It is said, for the person of the highest capacity and diligence, that dreams cease by being forgotten. For the intermediate person they cease by being recognized. For the person of a lesser capacity they cease through the experience of excellent dreams.

For people of the highest capacity, dreams dissolve into emptiness and are forgotten. Intermediate people recognize dreams to be dreams, after which they stop. People of lower capacity only have good dreams, after which they stop. These are the different types of experience you might have.

The fact that dreaming must be purified in the end is commonly agreed upon in all the sutras, tantras, and treatises.

We do need to purify our dreams, as talked about in all the sutras, tantras, and treatises. In Khenpo Gangshar's shorter instructions, he calls this instruction taking delusion as the path. When we talk about delusion in general, we normally mean the delusion included among the three poisons of greed, aversion, and delusion. Delusion has the aspect of not knowing and misunderstanding—not knowing the way the dharma nature is, being ignorant of karma, cause, and effect. But that is not what Khenpo Gangshar means when he talks of taking delusion as the path. Because sleep is considered a kind of ignorance, he means taking sleep as the path.

When we are going to sleep, it is important not to let our minds be overcome by distraction. We need to be as mindful and aware as we can and to try to rest our minds naturally in the essence of mind. If we can do this as we fall asleep, our sleep will become clearer and clearer; our dreams will become clearer and clearer. In the best of cases, when we wake up in the morning we will awaken within the nature of the mind itself. This is perhaps difficult, but if we can be mindful and aware first when we are falling asleep and then while we are sleeping, when we wake up we will be able to take it as the path.

Next, Khenpo Gangshar mentions that the instructions on the practice of phowa have points that relate to taking the bardo as the path.

> The additional points about the practice of phowa should
> be learned from other sources.

Sometimes when we are practicing, we might suddenly encounter obstacles in our lives. At that time, as a method to avoid falling into the lower realms of samsara, there are the instructions on phowa. There are many additional instructions on the practice of phowa, but they are not taught here; you should learn them from other sources. The instruction here is to just rest in equipoise within the coemergent mind.

The method for taking all situations as the path is to rest within the essence of the mind. Within our minds, there are three aspects: the way things appear, how they are confused, and the way they actually are. We do not take our difficulties as the path in relation to how things appear or are confused, but in relation to how they actually are. We rest naturally within their nature—the clear and empty nature of the mind that is sometimes called the union of clarity and emptiness or the union of wisdom and the expanse. We rest within this, recognizing it. When we take sickness as the path, we look at the essence of the sickness without altering it in any way and just rest naturally within that. When we take the afflictions as the path, we just look at the essence of the greed, aversion, or delusion that has occurred. We do not follow the affliction or block it. We do not try to stop our thoughts. Instead, we look at those thoughts and at the afflictions that occur, and we rest naturally within their inherently empty essence. When we take the bardo as the path, the natural light and resonance of the dharma nature appear, and we rest in equipoise within those, not altering them in any way at all. When we take sleep as the path, we rest within whatever appearances occur in our sleep, relaxing the mind without altering it. The heart of all of these applications is to rest naturally in the nature of the mind.

Resting in the nature of the mind is not just the heart of the applications. The preliminary stage of the analytic meditation of the pandita is a method to develop realization while resting within the natural state. Resting in the mind-essence is also the essence of the main practice, the resting meditation of the kusulu. Simply resting in the nature of mind without altering anything is a way to develop ultimate experience within ourselves. The essence of taking situations as the path is also to rest in meditation within the unaltered essence of the mind. In this way, all of these practices come down to this same important point: the main method is to just let yourself settle naturally into the essence of your mind.

18

CLOSING WORDS

KHENPO GANGSHAR'S instructions close with some verses of summary and an aspiration prayer:

These teachings were merely a condensation of the basic points of the instructions.

From the core of realization of all the victorious ones
and their sons,
The root advice of the profound points of the new and
old tantras,
I have extracted the fresh essence of the profound oral
instructions
And written them down concisely in a few words.

These instructions are a digest that combines all the key points from the instructions of the buddhas and bodhisattvas—the victorious ones and their children—as well as from the tantras of the Nyingma and Sarma traditions. This text also takes the pith of the profound oral instructions and presents all of these in a brief and concise manner.

It is taught that in these times when it is difficult to tame
beings through the vehicles of effort,
The teachings of effortless mind will appear.
By the power of the times, if you practice these points,
They are a teaching that is easy to apply and devoid
of error.

Many different instructions and practices require a lot of effort, preparation, and ritual, but we cannot always practice these instructions. At such times, we need effortless instructions such as these that are easy to practice and have few spots where we could go wrong.

> At a time when I saw many reasons
> And was also requested by several eminent people,
> Setting aside elaborate poetry and lengthy expressions,
> This was written by Gangshar Wangpo, a khenpo from
>   Shechen,
> Naturally and freely, in a way that is pleasant to hear and
>   easy to understand.

This was written in a simple style that is meant to be easily understood. It uses common, ordinary language rather than high philosophical language with flowery, eloquent expressions. If for that reason, some of his words are not quite right, that is not so important. What is really important is that we have instructions that are beneficial and given in a way that is easy to understand.

> By the virtue of this, may an infinite number of beings
> Be victorious in the battle with the demigods of platitude,
> May they shine with the majestic brilliance of the essence
>   of profound meaning
> And may there be a celebration of a new golden age.

These are times when there will be difficulties, strife, and danger, and many negative thoughts and afflictions will run through our minds. May we realize the meaning of these teachings and bring great happiness to the world.

These teachings are very powerful and helpful. We really need to know how to take all of the situations of our lives—joy and sorrow, the afflictions, illness, and the bardo—as the path. The instructions on doing this will help us a great deal. That is why it is important to prepare and practice doing them now. If this practice were extremely difficult, requiring a lot of effort and involving many complicated things, not many people would be able to do it. But the analytic meditation of the pandita and the resting meditation of the kusulu do not require much effort either physically or mentally. If you want to make a lot of effort to practice them, that is great, but strenuous effort is not necessary. These practices are easy to do, which makes them helpful in times of difficulties.

What is most important is to be able to practice these instructions. That is not only necessary, it is also beneficial. In this human life we are happy at times, joyful at times—we have no problems and everything goes well. At such times, we should not let our attention be drawn away and be overcome by distraction: we need to remember the experience of naturally resting in the essence of mind. If we can nurture this experience, it will be helpful. At times in our lives it is possible that we will have problems and difficulties. We will experience pain and illness, the afflictions, and the bardo. These happen to every single living being, so we need a way to deal with them. At such times we should not let ourselves be overwhelmed by the situations in our lives. If in those times we are able to remember how to rest in the natural state, the practice will help ease us through our difficulties. Whatever we do in this human life, it is important to remember to be mindful, aware, and careful, and to rest in the essence of how things are. If you can practice these instructions, they will gradually bring you many benefits. The more you practice them, the more helpful they will be.

But they are not just helpful in and of themselves: we actually need to put some effort into them. We actually need to put them into practice. There is a Tibetan saying, "When you walk in the fields, you sing *tra la la la la.* When you go into the dark cave, you pray to Guru Rinpoche." If just you sing merry songs to yourself when everything is fine and then start saying "Guru Rinpoche, Guru Rinpoche" when you encounter a difficult situation, that is too little, too late. If you start practicing when things are good, when things turn bad you will be better able to handle it. This is why it is important to start practicing these instructions now.

That is the key point. For example, if you are sitting at a table with a plate of delicious food in front of you, you don't think, "How should I eat this? If I eat this, what will happen in my stomach?" There's no need to analyze it logically. Instead, you just eat and fill your belly. Then your body will feel comfortable. Similarly, it is important to actually practice and not just think conceptually about these instructions.

The most important thing is to be as diligent as possible. If we can practice with diligence and we encounter no insurmountable obstacles, we are very fortunate. There is no way to be too diligent about Dharma practice—you cannot practice too much. The more you practice, the more it will help you. Such a situation is a wonderful opportunity. But our lives do not always permit this. Sometimes you might not have all the right circumstances for practice, or you might face difficulties or find yourself in an adverse situation. This can happen, and when it does, you should not worry that you cannot practice—there is no reason to worry or be depressed. You should not think, "Oh poor me! I can't practice Dharma!" That will not help. Actually you need to remember that you are extremely fortunate to have entered the gate of the Dharma and developed faith and devotion. This alone is a great merit; this alone is a great fortune. It actually is quite wonderful.

The Buddha himself taught this in a sutra. If someone feels strong faith and devotion, and joins their two hands at their heart in prayer, this will bring a great result. It is necessary and beneficial. But what if someone who thinks, "Well, Dharma is probably okay," but is doubtful and ambivalent about it raises a single hand to their heart even without much sincerity or faith, does this have any result? The Buddha said that it does. Even raising just a single hand in prayer is a great merit and a great fortune. The reason is that we have been wandering through samsara since beginningless time, and we have never felt much faith or excitement about the Dharma. Raising just one hand is the beginning of developing faith, conviction, and excitement about the Dharma. It will make good imprints within that person, and in the future those imprints will grow stronger and stronger, ultimately leading to great results. Here we are talking about not merely raising a hand to the heart but actually doing meditation practice. This is an especially good fortune!

APPENDIX
THE TEXTS OF KHENPO GANGSHAR

WHAT FOLLOWS ARE THE TWO TEXTS BY KHENPO GANGSHAR referred to in the text. First are the short instructions, "The Concise Mind Instructions Called Naturally Liberating Whatever You Meet," written by Khenpo Gangshar in August of 1957 while he was visiting Thrangu Monastery in Tibet. In 2005, a handwritten copy of these instructions was found in Thrangu Rinpoche's personal library, from which this translation was prepared.

The second text is the slightly longer "Naturally Liberating Whatever You Meet: Instructions to Guide You on the Profound Path." It was written a few weeks after the "Concise Mind Instructions" and explains in greater detail the points made briefly there. It was translated by Erik Pema Kunsang and published in *The Crystal Cave* (Rangjung Yeshe Publications). It has been revised for this volume in cooperation with Erik Pema Kunsang.

— DAVID KARMA CHOEPHEL

The Concise Mind Instructions Called
Naturally Liberating Whatever You Meet

IF YOU DO VIRTUOUS ACTIONS, happiness will result, and if you do unvirtuous actions, suffering will result. This is an unfailing fact, so we must identify what we call virtue and misdeed. In order to do that, we first need to point out what body, speech, and mind are. After recognizing what those are, we need to know which is most important in virtues and misdeeds: body, speech, or mind.

If you ask which is most important, mind is most important. As it is said:

> The body is a servant for all good or evil deeds;
> The mind rules over everything like a king.

The mind is like the king, and the body and speech are like servants. Thus if the mind does not think of something, the body cannot possibly do anything either good or nasty, nor can the speech possibly say anything kind or mean. Thus we must recognize that the root comes down to the mind.

Next we must analyze whether the mind is something or nothing. It is not unilaterally something, because it has no color—white, yellow, red, or green—and no shape—triangular or square—to be seen. It is not unilaterally nothing, because this all-knowing, all-aware king that does all your thinking and remembering is unceasing. Thus as the glorious Rangjung Dorje said,

> Not something, even the victors cannot see it.
> Not nothing, it is the ground of all samsara and nirvana.

This completes the discussion of the preliminaries.

For the main practice, let the mind and body be comfortable, soft, and relaxed. Do not think of anything, let yourself settle naturally, and look up with your eyes into space. Open your mouth slightly and let the breath flow naturally. At that point, without any concern about what you are thinking, what you remember, what is nice or what is painful, this mind-essence is clear and expansive, vivid and naked. This is the nature of the minds of all sentient beings of the three realms. This is the heart of the glorious master, the supreme guide. This is what the buddhas of the three times intend. It is also called the dharmakaya mahamudra. It is also called the luminous great perfection. It is also called the path and result. It is also called emptiness and compassion. It can be given many names, but they all point a finger at just this.

Thus it is as the glorious Rangjung Dorje said,

> Everything's not true, not false,
> Like moons in water, say the wise.
> This ordinary mind itself
> Is dharma expanse, the victors' essence.

Directly, whatever arises, do not change it—rest naturally. This fulfills the essence of all creation stages, completion stages, mantra recitations, and meditations.

Here you must differentiate between being distracted and not being distracted. If you are undistracted and natural, there can be neither help nor harm. That is awareness. If you get slightly distracted, it is possible that likes or dislikes might arise in your mind. On top of that, you accumulate white or black karma. Because of that, you wander in samsara. For this reason you must distinguish mind and awareness. Mind and thought are like cloud banks and must be purified. You must rely on inner awareness.

You must take sickness as the path, afflictions as the path, the bardo as the path, and delusion as the path. The heart of all these applications is to rest naturally in the essence.

There's no need to bore you now.

This was kindly given by Gangshar Wangpo, who is both learned and accomplished, to the assembled students of Thrangu Tashi Chöling's school Shedrup Dargye Ling on the seventh day of the sixth month of the Fire-Bird year (August 3, 1957). Mangalam. Translated by David Karma Choephel in Boudhanath, Nepal, March, 2007.

Naturally Liberating Whatever You Meet:
Instructions to Guide You on the Profound Path

WITH THE DEVOTION of self-knowing I pay homage to Guru Vajradhara.

A worthy student is one who aspires to practice the profoundest of the profound and secret vajrayana—the essential oral instructions of all the anuttara yoga tantras or the nature of the realization of effortless ati. To meet the needs of such a student, these three points should be taught:

- The preliminary steps of mind training.
- The main practice of pointing out.
- The subsequent application, combining the profound advice into key points.

The first of these is in two parts: the general preliminaries and the special preliminaries, which represent the unique qualities of this particular path.

THE GENERAL PRELIMINARIES

First of all, you should practice the following steps according to the general teachings:

- Taking refuge, which is the difference between this path and an incorrect path.
- Arousing bodhichitta, which raises you above the inferior paths.

- The meditation and recitation of Vajrasattva, which purifies misdeeds, obscurations, and adverse conditions that prevent the essence of refuge and bodhichitta from dawning in your being.
- The mandala offering, which is the method for gathering the accumulations—the harmonious conditions.
- Guru yoga, the root of blessings and the means by which the special qualities of experience and realization quickly arise in your being.

THE SPECIAL PRELIMINARIES

Next, the special preliminaries, which, according to this system of teachings, are called the *analytic meditation of a pandita*.

It is an unfailing fact that happiness results from virtuous action and that suffering results from having committed unvirtuous karmic deeds. Therefore, you must first recognize what is virtuous and what is evil. In order to do this you must determine which is most important: your body, speech, or mind. To decide this, you must understand what your body, speech, and mind are.

The "body" is your physical body that serves as the support for benefit and for harm. "Speech" is the making of sounds and talking. The "mind" is that which can think of and recollect anything at all—that which feels like or dislike and at every moment shows different expressions of joy and sorrow. This briefly explains the body, speech, and mind.

When you commit a virtuous or evil action, you must ask yourself, "Is the body the main thing? Is speech the primary aspect? Or is the mind most important?" Some people will reply that it is the body, some that it is speech, and some will say that the mind is the primary aspect. In any case, whoever claims that the body or speech is most important has not really penetrated to the core with their examination.

It is the mind that is the most important. The reason is that unless your mind intends to do so, your body cannot possibly do anything good or bad. Nor can your voice express anything good or evil. Your mind is therefore the primary factor. As it is said,

The mind rules over everything like a king,
The body is a servant for all good or evil deeds.

In that way your mind is like a king and both your body and speech are its servants. For instance, when you get angry at your enemy you must examine whether the primary factor is your mind or the enemy. Similarly, when you feel attached to a friend, examine whether your mind or the friend is the primary factor. Examining in this way, you must acknowledge that although the friend and enemy are the circumstances in which attachment and anger arise, the real cause originates in your own mind. Thus, your mind is most important.

Once you master you own mind, neither friend nor enemy will be able to benefit you or cause you harm. If you don't gain control over your mind, attachment and anger will automatically well up, wherever you go and wherever you stay. You must understand that your mind is the root of all joy and sorrow, good and evil, attachment and anger. The Great Omniscient One (Longchenpa) has said,

> When under the influence of dhatura,
> All the various experiences you have, whatever they
>   may be,
> Are all, in fact, mistaken images without existence.
> Likewise, understand that under the influence of a
>   confused mind
> All the mistaken experiences of the six classes of beings,
>   whatever they may be,
> Are all empty images, nonexistent yet appearing.
> Since they appear in your mind and are constructed by
>   your mind,
> Exert yourself in taming this mistaken mind.

That is how it is. But you shouldn't take your understanding from books or stories heard from others. Recognize, yourself, that appearance is mind and understand that your mind is the root of all phenomena.

In this context, you must distinguish between appearance (*nangwa*) and the perceived object (*nang-yul*). Without doing that, it will be like the Great Omniscient One stated,

> Ignorant people claim that everything is mind.
> They are deluded about the three types of appearance,
> Have many shortcomings, mix things up and overexaggerate.
> Meditators, give up such unwholesome ways!

The mere presence of visible forms, sounds, and so forth, that are the objects of the six types of consciousness is called "perceived objects." Thoughts of attachment, anger, or delusion based on the "perceived objects" are "appearances," for example, the feeling of attachment to a pleasant object, the feeling of anger toward an unpleasant one and the indifferent feeling toward something neutral. You must understand that such appearances are the functions of your own mind.

Perceived objects, such as form, sound, and so forth, have appeared due to mind, but they are not mind—they are the shared appearances of sentient beings and do not possess any true existence, besides being phenomena of dependent origination.

You should now examine where this mind dwells: from the top of the hair on your head to the nails on your toes; from the outer layer of skin, the flesh in between, to the bones, five organs, and six vessels within. When investigating the dwelling place of mind, most Chinese will claim that it abides in the head. Tibetans will say that it dwells in the heart. Neither one is sure because when you touch the top of the head the mind seems to leap there and when you touch the soles of the feet it seems to jump there. It has no fixed place. It dwells neither in outer objects nor inside the body, nor in the empty space in between. You must become certain that it has no dwelling place.

If your mind has a dwelling place, what are the outer, inner, and middle aspects of this dwelling place? Is it identical with or different from the dweller?

If they are identical—since there is increase or decrease, change and alteration in outer objects and within the body—your mind will change in the very same way. So it is illogical to think they are identical.

If they are different, then is the essence of this different mind something that exists or not? If it is, then it should at least have a shape and color. Since there is no shape or color, it does not unilaterally exist. However, since this "Ever-conscious and Ever-aware King" is unceasing, it does not unilaterally not exist. For this reason the glorious Karmapa Rangjung Dorje proclaimed,

> It is not existent since even the victorious ones do not
> see it.
> It is not nonexistent since it is the basis of samsara and
> nirvana.
> This is not a contradiction, but the middle way of unity.
> May we realize the nature of mind, free from extremes.

The explanation up to this point completes the preliminary teachings of the *analytical meditation of a pandita.*

THE MAIN PART OF THE PRACTICE

The second part, the steps of the teachings on the main part of the practice, the *resting meditation of a kusulu,* is presented under two points:

- Pointing out the nature of body, speech, and mind by means of the instruction in *resolving.*
- Pointing out (dualistic) mind and awareness, one by one, by means of the instruction in *distinguishing.*

RESOLVING

Keep your body straight, refrain from talking, open your mouth slightly, and let the breath flow naturally.

Don't pursue the past and don't invite the future. Simply rest naturally in the naked ordinary mind of the immediate present without trying to correct it or "re-place" it. If you rest like that, your mind-essence is clear and expansive, vivid and naked, without any concerns about thought or recollection, joy or pain. That is awareness (*rigpa*).

At the same time, there is no thought of, "Sights and sounds are out there." Everything appears unceasingly. There is also no thought of, "The perceiver, the six types of consciousness, is within." Clear and nonconceptual naked awareness is unceasing.

While in that state, your body is left to itself without fabrication, free and easy. That is the body of all the victorious ones. That is the essence of the creation stage.

Your speech is free from fabrication, without efforts to track down the root of sound but simply expressing directly and openly whatever comes to mind. It is all-pervasive from the very moment of being heard, a nonarising empty resounding. That is the speech of all the victorious ones. It is the essence of all recitation.

When you rest your mind in unfabricated naturalness, no matter what thought may arise, good or evil, happy or sad, the mind-essence, which is free from concerns about joy or sorrow, is clear and empty, naked and awake.

This mind-essence is the nature of all sentient beings, the realization of the buddhas of the three times, the essence of the eighty-four thousand Dharma-doors and the heart of the glorious master, the supreme guide. It is the transcendent knowledge of the second set of teachings and the sugata-essence of the last turning of the wheel of the Dharma. According to the general system of mantra it is called *continuity of ground*, the spontaneously present mandala of the innate nature. According to the anuttara tantras it is called Guhyasamaja, Chakrasamvara, Kalachakra, and so forth.

As for the three inner tantras: according to mahayoga, it is the great dharmakaya of the exalted inseparability of the two truths. According to anuyoga, it is the basic mandala of bodhichitta of the "son of great bliss." According to atiyoga, it is the great perfection of awareness and emptiness.

All these renowned expressions point a finger at this mind-essence itself, and nothing else. This point is also presented in the Gelug school, as stated by the Great Lord (Tsongkhapa),

Appearance, the unfailing dependent origination,
And emptiness, understanding beyond statements—
As long as these two seem to be separate,
You have still not realized the intent of Shakyamuni.
When all at once and without alternation
Your conviction and your notion of an object fall apart,
That is the moment of having completed the analysis
    of the view.

The Lord of Dharma, Drakpa Gyaltsen, has said,

When you have clinging, it is not the view.

The Dharma masters of the Sakya school regard their view of undivided samsara and nirvana to be nonfixation. Moreover, according to the matchless Kagyupa masters, glorious Rangjung Dorje proclaimed,

Everything's not true, not false,
Like moons in water, say the wise.
This ordinary mind itself
Is dharma expanse, the victors' essence.

Thus, the luminous mahamudra is also nonfixation. It is said that all the learned and accomplished masters of India and Tibet had the same realization and there is not a single master who claims that the realization of the main part of practice is anything other than nonfixation. That is the meaning you should understand yourself and what you should point out to others.

This completes the section that indicates that your body, speech, and mind are the Body, Speech, and Mind (of the victorious ones). It has the same meaning as in the verses by the Great Master of Uddiyana, beginning with, "Do this toward all that you see," and so forth.

DISTINGUISHING

It is very important to distinguish the difference between mind (*sem*) and awareness (*rigpa*). The Great Omniscient One said,

The big oxen pretending to know ati nowadays
Claim that discursive thinking is awakened mind.
Such ignorant people, in their realm of darkness,
Are far away from the meaning of the natural
    Great Perfection.

If you fail to distinguish between mind and awareness you may engage in conduct that confuses cause and result and thus turn away from the path in which view and conduct are united.

When experiencing the continuity of undistracted naturalness, awareness is free from a reference point, like sky, without even a speck of joy or sorrow, hope or fear, benefit or harm, whether you meet with positive or negative conditions. The character of (dualistic) mind is evident the moment you get slightly distracted and encounter (the same) conditions and you feel joy or sorrow. Having given rise to joy or sorrow, you will accumulate karmic actions.

For example, mind (*sem*) is like the clouds gathering in the sky. Therefore, you must gain stability in awareness (*rigpa*), which is like a cloudless sky. You must be able to purify the aspect of mind that is like the clouds in the sky.

Through this you will be able to separate mind and awareness.

THE PROFOUND ADVICE

The third part explains the profound advice on the subsequent application, which is based on the oral instructions that reveal direct self-liberation.

While you remain in undistracted naturalness it is utterly impossible to accumulate karma and you have cut the stream of the further accumulation of karma. Although you are not accumulating (new) karma, do not get the idea that there is neither good nor evil to be experienced as (past) karma ripens. That is, unless you purify all the karmic deeds you have previously accumulated through confession, purification, and so forth, they will ripen without fail. The ripening of karma is still possible.

This ripening will manifest in your body or mind and nowhere else. When it ripens in your body you will fall sick. When it ripens in your mind you will feel joy or sorrow and the thoughts of the six types of disturbing emotions will arise. When that happens, it is important to possess the oral instructions on taking sickness as the path, taking joy and sorrow as the path, taking disturbing emotions as the path, and so forth. But, if you simply rest in naturalness, the essence of all these applications, it will suffice.

If you feel happy when meeting with good conditions and sad when encountering negative circumstances and indulge in the feeling of happiness when happy and the feeling of sadness when sad, you will accumulate immense karma. Therefore, you must immediately recognize a thought, be it happy or sad, in any circumstances, positive or negative.

After recognition, you should rest in naturalness. Look into the one who feels happy or sad, without repressing one feeling or encouraging the other. Your clear, empty, and naked mind-essence, free from any concern about joy or sorrow, freely becomes the innate state of awareness.

Furthermore, when your body falls sick, don't indulge in the illness, but rest in naturalness. Look into the painful sensation itself. The pain doesn't cease when resting like that. However, you will directly realize the innate state of awareness free from any thought about where it hurts, what hurts, how it hurts, as well as the subject and object of the pain. At that moment the sickness grows less intense and becomes somewhat insubstantial.

A person who has one disturbing emotion will also possess the others. But due to the differences in people, some will have more anger, some more stinginess, some more dullness, some more desire, some more envy, and some will have a greater portion of pride. That is why there are different types of buddha families.

The disturbing emotion of anger is an agitated state of mind caused by a painful sensation based on an unpleasant object.

Stinginess is the inability to give away to others some attractive object because of retaining a tight clinging to owning it.

Dullness is like darkness and is the root of all evil. It is the lack of recognizing one's essence and it obscures the nature of things.

Desire is to accept, long for, and feel attached to pleasant things like sights or sounds and so forth. In particular, carnal lust for the union of male and female is the primary attachment.

Envy is to reject and therefore disapprove of the virtues of someone who is higher than or equal to oneself.

Pride is to regard others as lower and to feel superior in either religious or mundane matters.

These six disturbing emotions create the causes for the existence of the six classes of beings, such as rebirth in the hells through predominant anger. Whenever one of them arises you must recognize it immediately. When recognizing it, don't reject it, don't accept it, just rest in naturalness [looking] into that particular disturbing emotion. At that same moment it is self-liberated and is called mirror-like wisdom, etc. This is mentioned in a song from the *Second Treasury* of Ratna Lingpa:

> The essence of your angry mind is clear awareness,
> Bright and empty the moment you recognize it.
> This nature is called mirror-like wisdom.
> Young maid, let's rest in the natural state.
>
> The essence of your dull mind is clear self-awareness,
> Wide open the moment you look into your natural face.
> This vital nature is called dharmadhatu wisdom.
> Young maid, let's rest in the natural state.
>
> The essence of your proud mind is the unfolding of
>   self-awareness,
> Naturally empty the moment you rest, looking into your
>   natural face.
> This state is called the wisdom of equality.
> Young maid, let's rest in the natural state.
>
> The essence of your lustful mind is attachment for sure,
> The state of empty bliss, the moment you sustain it
>   without clinging.
> This nature is called discriminating wisdom.
> Young maid, let's rest in the natural state.

That is how it is. But if you regard disturbing emotions as faults and reject them, they may be temporarily suppressed but not cut from their root. Consequently, at some point, the poisonous remnant will reemerge, as is the case of the mundane dhyana states. On the one hand, when you regard disturbing emotions as emptiness, your practice turns into "taking emptiness as the path" and not the disturbing emotions. Thus your practice doesn't become the short path, the special quality of mantra. On the other hand, if you indulge in the disturbing emotions, thinking they are something concrete, it is like eating a poisonous plant and is the cause that binds you to samsara, just like the copulation of ordinary people.

For these reasons, just as poison can be extracted from a poisonous plant and taken as a medicine, the special quality of this teaching lies in the fact that any disturbing emotion that may arise is wisdom the moment you relax in naturalness. Look directly into it, don't deliberately reject it, regard it as a fault, indulge in it concretely, or regard it as a virtue.

Beyond this, if you are interested in the system of direct instructions, such as the teachings on the *path of means,* you must learn them in detail from the oral instructions of your master.

Taking the Bardo State as the Path

When you press your fingers on your ears or on your eyes, sounds naturally resound and colors and lights naturally manifest. Rest naturally for a long time and grow accustomed to the appearance of utterly empty forms that don't exist anywhere—neither outside, inside, nor in between. Since, at the time of death, there is nothing other than this, you will recognize these sounds, colors, and lights as your self-display and be liberated, just like meeting a person you already know or a child leaping onto its mother's lap.

This teaching corresponds to the key point of darkness instruction among the *daylight instructions* and *darkness instructions* for practicing the manifest aspect of the thögal of spontaneous presence. There are also the systems of practice based on the rising and setting rays at daytime and on the moonlight, electric light and lamps at nighttime.

Taking Sleep as the Path

Without depending on mental effort, such as emanations or trans-formations during the dream state, sleep in a state of undistracted naturalness. During that time, you may slip into deep sleep devoid of dreams. As soon as you awake you are vividly clear in the natural state. This is called the *luminosity of deep sleep*.

It may happen that sleep doesn't occur at all. Instead, you remain awake and vividly clear or you fall asleep. But, though various dreams take place, they are forgotten the moment you wake up the next morning with nothing to remember. That is the beginning of having purified dreams.

It is said, for the person of the highest capacity and diligence, that dreams cease by being forgotten. For the intermediate person they cease by being recognized. For the person of a lesser capacity they cease through the experience of excellent dreams. The fact that dream-ing must be purified in the end is commonly agreed upon in all the sutras, tantras, and treatises.

The additional points about the practice of phowa should be learned from other sources.

These teachings were merely a condensation of the basic points of the instructions.

> From the core of realization of all the victorious ones and
>   their sons,
> The root advice of the profound points of the new and
>   old tantras,
> I have extracted the fresh essence of the profound oral
>   instructions
> And written them down concisely in a few words.
> It is taught that in these times when it is difficult to tame
>   beings through the vehicles of effort,
> The teachings of effortless mind will appear.
> By the power of the times, if you practice these points,
> They are a teaching that is easy to apply and devoid
>   of error.

At a time when I saw many reasons
And was also requested by several eminent people,
Setting aside elaborate poetry and lengthy expressions,
This was written by Gangshar Wangpo, a khenpo from
    Shechen,
Naturally and freely, in a way that is pleasant to hear and
    easy to understand.

By the virtue of this, may an infinite number of beings
Be victorious in the battle with the demigods of platitude,
May they shine with the majestic brilliance of the essence
    of profound meaning
And may there be a celebration of a new golden age.

Sarva dakalayanam bhavantu

*Translated in accordance with the oral teachings of Tulku
Urgyen Rinpoche at Nagi Gompa, 1984, by Erik Pema
Kunsang. Edited by Ward Brisick, 1989. Revised 2009.*

Bibliography

The Hundred Thousand Songs of Milarepa (Tsang Nyon Heruka). Author's own translation.

The Third Karmapa Rangjung Dorje. "The Aspiration Prayer of the Mahamudra of Definitive Meaning." *The Kagyu Monlam Book*. 2nd edition. Woodstock, N.Y.: KTD Publications, 2010.

———. "A Treatise on Buddha Nature." In *On Buddha Essence* by Khenchen Thrangu. Boston: Shambhala Publications, 2006. In Tibetan, *karmapa rang byung rdo rje'I gsung 'bum*. Vol. 7, 289–98. zi ling: tshur phu mkhan po lo yag bkra shis, 2006.

Padmakara Translation Group, trans. *The Way of the Bodhisattva*. By Shantideva. Revised edition. Boston: Shambhala Publications, 2006.

Sakya Pandita Kun dga' rgyal mtshan. *Treasure of Valid Logic (tshad ma rig gter)*. Chapter 4, "The Chapter on the Examination of Proofs and Exclusions." bod ljongs mi dmangs dpe skrun khang, 1989.

Index

abhidharma, 46, 98
accumulation of merit and wisdom, 39–40
afflicted mind. *See* consciousness: afflicted mind
affliction(s), 72, 81, 124, 138, 183, 188, 189, 200–201
    buddha families and, 184, 229
    cause of, 16, 68–69, 88, 172
    emotions not included in, 182–83, 197
    emptiness and, 71, 183–84, 189–90, 195
    indulging in, 195–96
    Ratna Lingpa's instructions on, 191–94
    suppressing, 194–95
    taken as the path, 173–74, 182–94, 196–97, 208, 218, 229–31
    three methods for dealing with, 194–96
    See also poisons
afflictive obscurations. *See* obscurations: afflictive and cognitive
aggregate of consciousness, 98
aggregate of formations, 98–99
ālaya. See consciousness: all-ground
all-ground. *See* consciousness: all-ground
analytic meditation of a pandita, 43–112, 222–25
    direct perception and, 108–9

differing from middle-way logic, 94, 96–97
    differing from tranquility meditation, 120
    as a preliminary, 43–44, 209, 222
    seeing the nature of the mind in, 43–44, 107–8
    strenuous effort not necessary for, 211–12
    transcendent intelligence as goal of, 138–39
anger, 38, 124, 184, 188, 191, 229, 230
    definition of, 185
    mind as primary factor for, 60, 65, 85, 223–24
    taken as the path, 174, 183–84, 189–90
    See also aversion
anuttara yoga tantra. *See* unexcelled yoga tantra
anuyoga, 140, 226
appearances
    and dependent origination, 141–42, 172, 180, 227
    and emptiness, 103, 141–42, 151, 180, 227
    are mind, 20, 79–83, 92, 97, 102–3, 169, 224
    as differentiated from perceived objects, 83–85, 88, 90–93, 223–34
    in death and bardo, 200–202, 204
    three types of, 84–85, 224
ati, atiyoga, 22–23, 140, 159

resonance of the dharma nature, 202–6
resting in equipoise, 111–12, 126, 130, 133,
   144, 162, 206
resting in naturalness, 38, 135, 162,
   173–74, 177, 179, 206
resting meditation of a kusulu, 43–44,
   111–66, 173, 209, 211, 225
rigpa. *See* awareness (*rigpa*)

Sakya School, 139, 142–44, 227
Sakya Pandita, 86
samadhi
   Buddha in, 66–67
   hope and fear absent in, 162
   non-fixation and, 144
   purification of mind in, 164
   suppression of afflictions in, 195
   thoughts in, 135
   unceasing clarity in, 128
   See also equipoise
samsara, 9–10, 34, 188
   indivisibility from nirvana, 143, 227
   mind as basis of nirvana and, 104–5,
   217, 225
sangha, 35
Sarma, 5, 139, 210
scholars, 105, 144, 156–57
Second Treasury of Ratna Lingpa, 191,
   230
second wheel, 71–73, 137–38
secret mantra, secret mantra vajrayana.
   See vajrayana
self-awareness, 21, 77, 82, 86–87, 108, 192
self-aware direct perception, 108–9
self-clinging, clinging to a self, 68–70,
   148. *See also* ego-clinging.
self-empty school, 71–72
self-liberation, 169, 228, 230
selflessness, 10
   of phenomena, 16, 71, 136
   of the individual, 16, 68–71, 74–75, 136
sense consciousnesses. *See* consciousness: sense
sense faculties, 86, 88, 108, 128–29

senses, objects of, 83–93, 108, 128–29,
   148, 151, 186–87, 223–24
Seven Treasuries of Longchenpa, 79
seventh consciousness. *See* consciousness: afflicted mind
shamatha. *See* tranquility meditation
Shantideva, 26, 39, 63, 119, 183
Shechen Gyaltsap Gyurme Pema Namgyal, 6, 19
Shechen Kongtrul Rinpoche, 6–7, 19
Shechen Monastery, 6–7, 18
Short Vajradhara Lineage Prayer, 40, 113,
   129
sickness, 173, 179–81
six classes of beings, 188, 230
six consciousnesses. *See* consciousness:
   six
six transcendences, 73, 76
six yogas of Naropa, 22
sleep, 206–8
sound(s), 83–87, 90, 128–29, 147–50
speech, 50–51, 54–62, 133–34, 145, 151,
   222–23, 226
spontaneous presence, 82, 102–3, 142,
   169, 205, 226, 231
stability, 117–20
subsequent application, 30, 221
suffering, 34, 52, 64, 70
Supreme Continuum, The, 7, 126, 151–52
Surmang Dutsi Til monastery, 7, 12, 14
sutra(s), 40, 76, 95–96, 102, 123, 127,
   137–41, 213

Takpo Tashi Namgyal, 82, 146–47, 165,
   181
tantra(s), 22, 136, 138–40, 221, 226
Teachings on the Buddha Nature, 143,
   218, 227
termas. *See* treasures
tertöns, 11–12, 14, 190
Third Wheel, 73–75, 137–38
thögal, 22, 205, 231
Thrangu Monastery, ix, 12, 14–15, 18, 215
Three Jewels and Roots, 35